Hoomothya's Long Journey
1865 – 1897

The true story of a
Yavapai Indian

by Elaine Waterstrat

Mount McDowell Press
Fountain Hills, Arizona

Hoomothya's Long Journey □ *1865-1997* □ *The True Story of a Yavapai Indian*
Copyright © 1998 by Elaine Waterstrat
Printed and bound in the United States of America

Publisher: Mount McDowell Press, P.O. Box 17131, Fountain Hills, AZ 85269, (602) 837-2730

Book design by Elaine Waterstrat
Cover design by Kathryn Beegle
Cover paintings by Elaine Waterstrat
Photographs not otherwise credited are by Rodney Waterstrat
Maps by Kathryn Beegle and Elaine Waterstrat

Publisher's Cataloging-in-Publication Data
(Provided by Quality Books, Inc)

Waterstrat, Elaine.
    Hoomothya's long journey, 1865-1890 : the true story of a
  Yavapai Indian / by Elaine Waterstrat. -- 1st ed.
    p. cm.
    Includes bibliographical references and index.
    Preassigned LCCN: 97-94027
    ISBN: 0-9636649-1-3

  1. Hoomothya.   2. Yavapai Indians--Biography.   I. Title

  E99.Y5H66 1998   979.1'7300497'092 [B]
                                QB197-41032

Dedication

This book is dedicated to the descendants of the victims of the Salt River Cave Massacre
and to my grandchildren: Susan, Steven, James, Kaye, Joseph, Jacob, Virginia, Walter, Jonathan and Lillian.

Acknowledgments

Writing this book with historically accurate background and detail was possible because Mike Burns (Hoomothya) and his many contemporaries faithfully recorded their experiences. The Fountain Hills, Scottsdale and Mesa Public Libraries, the Fort McDowell Library, the Arizona State University Libraries, the Arizona State Capitol Library and Archives and the Sharlot Hall Museum Library graciously made these resources available for research and study.

Members of the Arizona Book Publishers Association (ABPA) shared their expertise for making my manuscript a viable product. Jack Carlson advised on layout and design of maps and text; Nathan Laskin and Eileen Birin helped in choosing a book manufacturer; Lisa Liddy, Sandi Lloyd, Paticia Troyer, and Janet Wandrey shared their thoughts on the cover art and design.

Members of the Fountain Hills Christian Writers Group, especially Naomi Burns, Effie Gross, Rosemary Malroy and Serena Wood, critiqued the first several chapters and provided encouragement over the past four years.

My friends and neighbors, authors and artists Charlotte Brown and Jean Thomsen read and critiqued the text and offered suggestions for the cover art.

My husband, Rod, proofread the text and traveled around the countryside taking photos. My daughter and son-in-law Katie and Jim Beegle designed the cover and scanned and perfected my sketched maps.

My readers and I are indebted to all the above.

Table of Contents

MAPS

PHOTOGRAPHS AND DRAWINGS

Foreward

"For a subject worked and reworked so often in novels, motion pictures and television, American Indians are probably the least understood and the most misunderstood Americans of us all." John F. Kennedy, 1963.

From the first page, *Hoomothya' Long Journey* quickly takes the romanticism of John Wayne western movies to gritty realism. The narrative and finite detail give the reader a realistic glimpse of the tremendous hardships and dangers endured by all people in the West during this period in recent history.

Foraging for food was a daily regimen. When Mike and his people were hungry, it seemed perfectly logical to eat rats, horse flesh and any available vegetation. Soldiers also had to struggle for food.

Western history usually has been portrayed as Indians versus soldiers and settlers. This book brings into focus the inter-tribal hostilities that often involved life and death struggles long before the white man came on the scene.

I was left with one prevailing thought about the Indian experience. Indians are survivors. Overall, life on the frontier was a grueling experience for everyone. The Indians who were under constant assault and threat of extermination suffered even greater miseries and indignities than the white men. They were killed with impunity because they had no recourse or legal standing in the country. In some parts of the country, bounties were paid for their extinction.

Human experience is at best precarious. Mike Burns survived because Captain James Burns had a flash of compassion for an Indian child at a time when such attitudes and feelings were not the norm. Within the context of the times, it seems highly unlikely that a career Army officer would include an Indian boy as part of his family and allow him to use his name as a family member.

Human life and destiny are subject to seemingly tiny insignificant incidents. An accident, a chance meeting or a decision based on intuitive instinct can change the course of a life in an instant. It seems a paradox that humans have been given the resolute will to control the general course of their lives and yet are subject to the whims of fate and the winds of change.

On a personal note I am a Chippewa Indian and identified with the narrative because many situations in Mike Burns' life are so like my own. It was almost uncanny. If I have read a book and it keeps reoccurring in my thoughts, then it is a good book. I read this book twice, so far.

George Russell
Phoenix, Arizona
March 1997

Author's Note: George Russell, an enrolled member of the Saginaw Chippewa Tribe, was born on the Isabella Indian Reservation in Mount Pleasant, Michigan. After his discharge from the United States Army in 1963, he pursued a successful career in civil engineering and construction in Arizona. In 1990 realizing that his knowledge of other Indians was limited, Russell began to research and organize demographic data. This effort resulted in two books, the *American Indian Digest* and *American Indian: Facts of Life* and a map of the *American Indian Nations* and Russell Publications.

Introduction

Hoomothya (Mike Burns) was first introduced to me in W. T. Corbusier's *Verde to San Carlos* nearly ten years ago as I researched the history of the Yavapai Indians—my neighbors who live on the Fort McDowell Yavapai Reservation northeast of Phoenix, Arizona. I met him again in Thomas Farish's *History of Arizona.*

I began to know Mike Burns as a real person after I located his manuscript in the Arizona Collection at the Arizona State University Library and studied his recollections of his childhood as Hoomothya and loss of his Yavapai family, his new identity as the adopted son of James Burns, his adventures and hardships as he scouted with Company G, Fifth Cavalry, his Eastern education and his return to Arizona and his people. Then I knew that I must share Mike's story with others by writing his biography.

After I had deciphered, organized and transcribed the manuscript and found help from other sources, the story of the first thirty-two years of Mike Burns' life evolved into a historically accurate narrative. All Mike's adventures are adapted from accounts in his manuscript, supplemented with information from other writers, especially his contemporaries—Doctor William and Fannie Corbusier, Thomas Farish, General George Crook, Captain John Bourke, Lieutenants Walter Schuyler and Charles King and others—and frequent injections of my interpretations and thoughts.

The description of the Salt River Cave Massacre is from John Bourke's first-hand account in *General Crook in Indian Country*. The many details of Mike's life at Camp Date Creek, which are missing in his manuscript, are from Corbusier. Sources for the Delche narrative include Averam Bender's *A Study of the Western Apaches*, General George Crook's, *Autobiography;* Farish's *History of Arizona*; Dan Thrapp's *Al Sieber: Chief of Scouts* and Edmund Wells' *Argonaut Tales*. The story of Pakotay's journey is adapted from Mike's manuscript, Corbusier's edited account in *Verde to San Carlos* and General Oliver Howard's *My Life and Experience Among Our Hostile Indians*. The events following the Wickenburg stage massacre are based largely on Charles Genung's account (Farish, Volume 8). Charles King's *Campaigning with Crook,* an officer's description of the Big Horn-Yellowstone Campaign, helped to fill gaps in Mike's narrative and put events in chronological order. King's account describes the final days of the foot brigade in the Black Hills—the events following the starvation march—which are absent from Mike's manuscript. Lieutenant Walter Schuyler's version of the starvation march as described in a letter to his parents (Crook's *Biography*) helped enrich the narrative in Chapters 22 and 23. Crook's narrative ends at the Rosebud. Constance Wynn Altshuler's *Cavalry Yellow and Infantry Blue* and Dan Thrapp's *Encyclopedia of Frontier Biography* provided biographical background for many army officers, Indian chiefs and other principals who influenced Mike's life.

Wanting the biography to be informative and of interest to researchers, history buffs, readers of fiction and other genres, my efforts were to have the story read smoothly, uninterrupted by notes. An index and bibliography appear at the end of the book. By writing in the first person, I hoped to keep the narrative—especially the extraordinary circumstances in which Mike found himself—believable and have his thoughts, moods and feelings, his humor and his pathos come across convincingly.

For nearly twenty years, Mike Burns tried unsuccessfully to publish his manuscript, sending out hundreds of typewritten copies to friends and publishers. Portions have appeared in Farish and Corbusier, but never before has his whole story been published. See page 249 of the epilogue. Finally, sixty-three years after his death, Mike Burns' remarkable story—the adventures of a young Yavapai and "the Indians' side of the story" is retold for all readers.

Elaine Waterstrat
Fountain Hills, Arizona
March 1997

Prologue
Arizona Indians

In 1863 Arizona Territory was Indian country. Three linguistic groups dominated the land.

Three to four thousand Yavapais occupied an area of approximately ten million acres in central and western Arizona. For centuries the Yavapais had roamed freely, eking out a living in the rugged mountain region of central Arizona—from the Superstitions to the red rock country of Sedona, from Tonto Creek to Bill Williams River. Yavapais often traveled 60 miles a day on foot. The seasons determined their temporary hunting and gathering sites and where the women constructed domed thatched. huts. They spoke a dialect of the Yuman language and were related to the Mohaves, Yumas, Havasupais and Hualapais. Before 1863 few white men had visited Yavapai country, and no white men stayed.

The Pimas, cousins of the Papagoes, had lived in villages along the Gila for hundreds of years. On irrigated fields they grew melons, squash, maize, cotton, beans, winter wheat, barley and other crops. The Pimas and the Papagoes were normally friendly toward one another, but they were always at war with the Athapascan speaking Apaches and Navajos, Yavapais who inhabited the mountain area north of the Gila River and the Yuman speaking tribes living along the Colorado River. There is one exception to the above. Early in the nineteenth century, the Yuman speaking Maricopas went to war with the Yumas and the Mohaves and resettled as neighbors and allies of the Pimas. For nearly fifty years, the Pimas and the white men had been friends. The Pimas provided protection against unfriendly Indians and kept many soldiers, prospectors and travelers from starving and thirsting to death in the Arizona wilderness. The Pimas provided wheat for the Confederate Army while it occupied their villages, and after the Union flag was raised over the trading post at Casa Blanca, they fed General Carleton's California Volunteers.

In 1863 there was no Phoenix, no Prescott, no Mesa. No white settlements existed north of the Gila River. South of the Gila, all white settlements except Tucson had been deserted and ravaged by the Apaches when the United States Army had left Arizona to fight the Civil War in the East.

In May 1863 the Walker party discovered gold on the Hassayampa River. The Yavapais hoped the intruders soon would find all the gold they wanted and leave central Arizona forever. They avoided clashes with the white men whose weapons were superior to their own. Unlike other Arizona tribes—particularly the Apaches and the Pimas— the Yavapais had no guns at this time. Most prospectors did not wish to start a war. They strove to live in peace with the people whose land they occupied; but they did not go away.

In the autumn of 1863, Fort Whipple was established to protect the two or three hundred prospectors and ranchers living in Central Arizona. In January 1864 officials for the new territorial government arrived, and in April—eleven months after the discovery of gold in central Arizona— Governor Goodwin located the capital of Prescott near the mining camps. Soon many immigrants from the East settled in and near the new capital. The new arrivals built homes and cleared the fields for farms—taking over lands previously occupied by the Yavapais. The Indians' precarious food supply was diminished, and they began to raid the corrals of the fort, the miners and the settlers. White men organized Indian hunts and shot any Indian on sight. Many Yavapais left the Prescott area to join other tribes in the Salt River and Tonto Creek wilderness.

In September 1865, Colonel Clarence Bennett established Fort McDowell on the west bank of the Verde, eight miles north of its confluence with the Salt, to control the Indians hiding in the nearby mountains and canyons. Three infantry companies of California Volunteers and two mounted and well-armed companies of Pima and Maricopa Indians—the first Arizona Volunteers—accompanied Bennett. Because the California Volunteers were occupied with post construction, their Indian allies did much of the scouting against the Yavapais.

When the troops went out on a scout and attacked an Indian village, the officers normally were not certain to which tribe the victims belonged or even if they were guilty of the crime for which they were punished. Most white men referred to all Indians as Apaches, the enemy. Others, confusing the Yavapais with both their Yuman speaking cousins and the more warlike Apaches, called them Apache-Mohaves or Apache-Yumas.

Into this environment, Hoomothya, a member of the Kwo-yo-ko-pa-ya tribe of Yavapais, was born. Many of Hoomothya's people would not survive; he was one of the fortunate ones.

Arizona Indians

Linguistic Group	Tribe
Yuman	Yavapai
	Havasupai
	Hualapai
	Mohave
	Yuma
Piman	Pima
	Papago
Athapascan	Apache
	Navajo

Yavapai (People of the Sun)

Kwo-yo-ko-pa-ya (Elsewhere People) =
    Southeastern Yavapai = Apache-Mohave
Tol-ko-pa-ya (Scrub Oak People) = Western
    Yavapai = Apache-Yuma
Wi-puk-a-pa-ya (People of the Red Rock Country)
    = Northeastern Yavapai

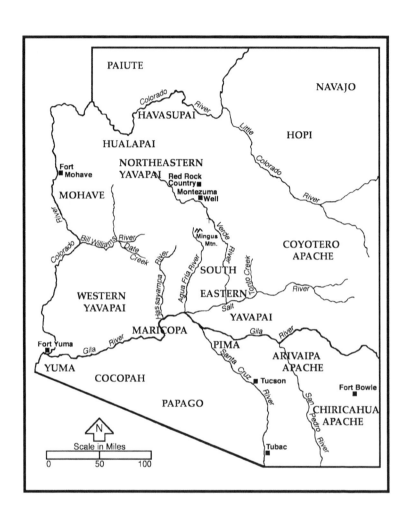

Arizona Indians 1863

Part I

Hoomothya
and His Family
1865 — 1872

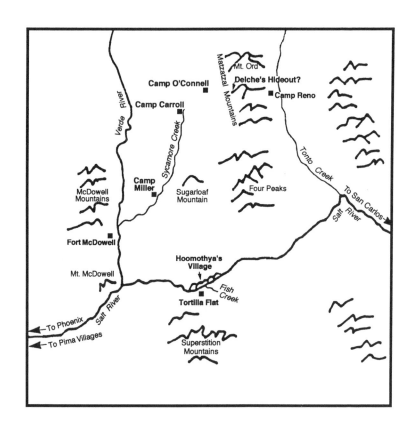

Hoomothya's World
1865-1872

1

Hoomothya

It is a mysterious thing that I am still living today, March 18, 1929, at Fort McDowell, Arizona, near the land where I was born and where the rest of my family died so long ago. It is a miracle that I can tell you how I was saved and that I can tell all that has happened to me and my family and to my people—that I can tell the Indian side of the story.

I cannot say exactly when or where I was born because my people could neither read nor write so they had no way to keep records of births or deaths. I cannot say just how old I am because I have no parents or near relatives to tell me when and where I was born. All my family was killed by soldiers in what is known as the "Bloody Salt River Cave Massacre" on December 28, 1872. Everyone else in my tribe who did not die at that time has since died. Just a few days before that terrible massacre, I was captured by Captain James Burns and Lieutenant Earl D. Thomas and Company G, Fifth United States Cavalry. The day of my capture, Lieutenant Thomas reckoned me to be seven or eight years old. That means I must now be sixty-four or sixty-five years old.

My Indian name is Hoo-mo-thy-a (Wet Nose), a name given to me at the time of my birth or when I was a very young child because, I think, my nose was covered with moisture. I probably was born in summer because I was once chosen to set fire to a mescal kiln. It was customary among my people to have a man or a woman or a boy or girl born in midsummer do this. They believed that if such a one started the fire, the mescal would cook just right and become sweet and juicy. If a young person not born in summer had started the mescal fire, it would not have cooked right. Instead, it would have turned out just as it was put in—green and hard to eat.

I remember the time I was called to light the fire. It was the last time my people all got together to make mescal, a very important food to my family and to all the Kwoyo-kopaya or Southeastern Yavapai. The white men called us Apache-Mohaves. Mescal came from the agave plant that grew on the eastern slopes of the hills above Fish Creek. When it was time to gather the agave, several bands from villages in the canyons and mountains near the Salt River and Tonto Creek came together for several weeks.

My father and most of the men and older boys were off hunting, but a few men stood guard over the camp as the women and the older girls prepared the mescal. Although I dreamed of the day I would join my father on the hunt, I was content to stand around with the other little children and watch our mothers. The women first dug a hole with sticks in the rocky soil about ten feet wide and three feet deep. My people did not have shovels or other metal tools until they lived on the reservation. It was hard work, but my mother never complained. The mescal would keep her family from starving during the winter when food would be less plentiful. When she had finished preparing the pit, it was time to gather the mesquite and oak for the fire. Although this was considered woman's work, I was so eager to light the fire that I was willing to help.

After cutting off the sharp pointed ends of the agave leaves, my mother piled the meatiest portions on the hot coals. Then she threw a layer of grass on top of the agave and poured water over the grass. I liked to be around to hear the first hissing sounds that meant it was time to cover the grass deep with soil. The mescal was left to cook for two or three days. I can still smell the wonderful aroma made by the roasting mescal. In those days when I was almost always hungry, I thought it was the best smell in the world.

When the dirt and grass were removed, a liquid, gooey, sticky stuff remained, which I thought was delicious. My mother picked up the stuff with her bare hands and placed it on a large flat rock in the direct sunlight. As the sun began to dry it, she began the hard work of kneading. I watched as she pushed, pounded and turned the hardening material. When the mescal had hardened enough, she shaped it into a large, dark, chewy cake about four inches thick that when nearly dry was ready to be stored and eaten for months to come. A small piece of mescal could keep up a man on a hunt for several days.

My earliest memories are of my home on the Salt River not far from where Fish Creek emptied its waters. Here the river raced and whirled through a canyon ten miles long and three miles wide. Walls fifteen hundred feet high rose above the canyon and kept out much sunlight. Many cave homes lay hidden among the rocks and precipices that stuck out from the high walls. My family's cave home was nearly half way up the canyon wall on the north side of the river. Here I lived in the winter with my parents, my little brother and sister, my grandparents, my aunt and uncle and their children.

In the summer my parents and I lived in a village of thatched domed huts, each about five feet high and seven feet wide, located in a secluded meadow a short distance below the cave. The women had built the huts. They first dug a hole with sharp sticks and with their bare hands, banking the earth around the hole until it was about one and a half feet deep. Around the hole they stuck branches of cottonwood trees that they bent over and fastened together to form a domed top thatched with grass. In cool weather the huts were covered with animal skins, but my family always moved into a cave in winter.

From the cave and my village home in the meadow, I could look down upon the canyon floor, but from the river bottom no one could see our cave or our village. There were only two paths, one across the mesa from the west and one from the southeast, where Indians who knew the way could climb the canyon wall from the river and reach first the village and then the cave by foot.

Farther up the canyon wall and above my family's cave home, the hidden fortress of Chief Nanni-Chaddi provided a popular place for powwows. Indians from other bands often assembled in the nearly circular area that lay in front of the large cave, which measured about one hundred feet wide and thirty-five feet deep. Steep rock steps—just wide enough for one man at a time—led to the cave. A natural, ten-feet high wall of stone protected the cave's entrance. Indians hidden behind the wall could throw a shower of rocks upon any enemy.

Often I led my nearly blind old grandfather around the caves in the canyon looking for rats' nests. I recall the day that I proudly carried six wood rats in the pouch that hung from my little waist As a child of about six, I was good at killing the small animals with a club. I could easily hit a quail with a rock, but that day we had seen no quails. "Our family eats well today," grandfather said smiling. He always skinned the larger animals, and my mother roasted them on an open fire. The smaller animals—skins and all—simmered in the family pot until tender. We ate the small pieces of meat and drank the liquid. Often relatives and guests arrived just in time to share our meal. Then no one had enough to eat, but no one starved to death either.

In the afternoon, Grandfather taught me how to make and set figure-four traps for catching rats, rabbits, and squirrels. Grandfather said, "We must rely on the animals' natural habits. We will use no bait, only a few seeds to attract the birds." The old man sent me to collect thistles that we placed around the traps to keep coyotes from stealing the trapped animals.

Before the sun disappeared behind the western walls of the canyon, we had set nearly fifty traps. "We will get up early to remove the animals," Grandfather said. "Then I will teach you to make a small bow and little arrows." I looked forward to another wonderful day.

That night the old man and several grandchildren gathered about the campfire. "Grandfather," I said, "tell us again why we are safe from our ancient enemies, the Pimas."

"Many summers ago," said Grandfather, "when Lofty Wanderer separated the bands, our people, the Kwoyokopaya, found their way to the Salt and Verde Rivers. Later, Pimas often came to our land. They attacked our people, burned our villages, and stole our children. So our people hid out in these rough and ragged mountains. When the Pimas entered the deep canyon, they were surprised by many great rocks tumbling from the sky. Seeing no human beings, they thought bad spirits threw the rocks. They ran out of the canyon as fast as possible and never returned."

"Do evil spirits live in these mountains, Grandfather?" I asked.

"No, my child. The rocks were hurled upon the Pimas by our people who kept out of sight. Since that time, we are always safe in our mountain hideout where no enemy can harm us."

"Do enemies ever find our people and steal little children?"

"Sometimes our people leave the mountains to gather seeds or summer fruits. They don't pay attention. Then the enemy attacks and kills. They capture little children and sell them to people who live far to the south. The enemy comes always at first light when everyone sleeps. We must always be careful when we are away from our canyon home."

Agave Plants Growing on the Hillside Near Fish Creek
Photo by Bonnie Kline

2

Kamalapukwia and Sakarakaamche

In the evening Grandfather often told his grandchildren stories about happenings before we were born, even before he was born. Our favorite was the Yavapai's creation story —the story of First Woman (Ka-ma-la-puk-wi-a) and her grandson, Lofty Wanderer (Sa-ka-ra-kaamche) and how the People of the Sun, the Yavapais, first came to be and live in this land. We loved that story, and we knew it by heart.

Many years before she was born, Kamalapukwia's ancestors had come up from the underworld on the first corn plant. No one from her tribe had ever left the big hole, now called Montezuma Well, Only Ihija, the dove, had one day flown up over the edge and seen the world. Kamalapukwia and her family were healthy and happy. Just enough sunshine and rain made the corn grow just right.

For weeks Gwi, the Cloud, had poured rain into the hole, and there was no escape for the people who lived there. "Only you can go to the outside world and be saved and start a new people," Kamalapukwia's father said to her.

Kamalapukwia would always remember the last moments before she set out on her dark and lonely journey away from the place that had always been her home. Years later she still saw the brave faces of her father and mother and the tearful one of her small brother. Her parents had told her to have courage, that all would be well. Then they had placed her and Ihija, the dove, with food for the journey—and the precious white stone—in the small log canoe. "You must keep the stone with you always," her mother warned. "Its power will keep you safe."

For many hours or perhaps days, Kamalapukwia was twirled and tossed about—somewhere in the unknown world. She had no way of knowing how long she lay there with only Ihija for company in her small dark boat. Then suddenly, her canoe came to a jolting halt as it hit solid earth. Kamalapukwia bumped her head so hard that the cover was shaken loose. She was finally free. Grasping the small white stone tightly, she crawled out of her dark prison into the misty air. Every part of her young body ached from long inactivity, and her head hurt from the bump she got when the boat landed. Her long and terrible and lonely voyage had brought her to safety, freedom and more loneliness.

With Ihija perched on her shoulder, Kamalapukwia slowly climbed Mingus Mountain to meet Nya, the Sun, as he came up from the other side of the mountain. When she reached the top, the eastern sky appeared to be on fire with reds and yellows. Having never before seen the rising sun, she was afraid. She freed Ihija and sat upon a rock to wait for Nya. The long climb had worn her out, and despite the cold and her anxiety she was soon asleep.

Nya, the Sun, came closer to the young woman. She is the only human being in the land, he thought, and she must be very lonely. I shall make her a child.

Kamalapukwia opened her eyes, but the glow from Nya blinded and frightened her. She closed her eyes. She felt warmer. The sun's warmth filled her whole body, and she became excited and afraid.

Nya said, "I am your friend; I love you and have made you my wife. I will tell you what to do. Now listen very carefully! You must not stay here. Winter will come soon, snow will cover the mountain, and you will find no food. You must go to the Red Rock country."

The young woman trembled in fear. "But how can I find the place?" she asked. "Where can I sleep? How can I find food?"

"Ihija will show you the way and will find a cave where you can make your home," Nya promised. "He will help you find food to eat and to store for the winter. Ihija will also keep you company. In a few months when I make the earth warm again, you will have a child to keep you from being lonely. You are the First Woman, but in a few years many tribes of people will live in the land."

Kamalapukwia was barely settled in her cave home in the red rock Country when the first snow came. She had never seen snow before as it was always warm at the bottom of the well. With Ihija's help she prepared for her first winter. The dove showed her where to find seeds, leaves, berries and insects that kept her alive and healthy the first few months, and she had stored a sufficient amount away for the winter. Nya told her how to make warm clothing and to build a fire. Much of the time, especially during the winter days when she could not leave her cave, she was lonely, but at least she was warm and well fed.

In the spring after Nya had warmed the earth, her little daughter was born. She named the child Am-ja-ku-poo-ka (Going Around on the Earth) as Nya had instructed. Kamalapukwia had no time for anxiety or loneliness. She spent all her waking hours tending the baby's every need and want and preparing for another winter.

Ihija stayed with her until spring. He flew off one day, and later made occasional visits with his new wife. After a few years, Kamalapukwia never saw him again. However, a large family of doves always roosted in the tall oak tree not far from her cave in Boynton Canyon. She believed the doves were Ihija's descendants.

As Amjakupooka grew, Kamalapukwia taught her daughter all she had learned from her parents, Nya and Ihija. The girl's only other companion was a friendly quail. One day Kamalapukwia persuaded her daughter to go to Mingus Mountain and ask Nya to give her a baby, but Nya recognized the girl as his own daughter and sent her to Gwi, the Cloud.

Amjakupooka named her son Sakarakaamche. The three of them—grandmother, daughter, and baby—were very content. They were never ill as there were no other humans around to give them diseases. The animals in their territory were friendly. They never forgot their magic stones. They were very happy—until one ill-fated day.

One day when the family had no green vegetables, Kamalapukwia asked her daughter to go to the river and gather watercress. Amjakupooka never returned.

Sakarakaamche was very lonely. Kamalapukwia, his grandmother, was especially busy today and had no time for him. He missed his mother who had played with him often and had always taken him with her when she had gone along the river looking for food. Then one day his mother had gone off alone, and he had never seen her again.

Sakarakaamche knew that his grandmother was very worried about her daughter's disappearance although she tried hard not to let her grandson know. He noticed Kamalapukwia's fright when she discovered that her daughter had left home without the white stone. She had always insisted that her daughter carry the stone for protection. When the little boy cried for his mother, his grandmother comforted him by singing to him and by telling him stories about the time before the flood when she had lived with her parents, little brother, grandparents, aunts and uncles and many cousins. Sakarakaamche thought that his grand-mother, who once lived with such a very large family, must be even more lonely than he.

Grandmother was always busy, collecting and preparing foods and herbs for the time when food would be hard to find. She taught her grandson to collect seeds, grasses and berries and how to make a small bow and arrows and to shoot small animals. The boy watched as she made bowls, jars and baskets from clay and grasses.

"Grandmother," he said to Kamalapukwia who was making him a shirt from small animal skins, "I am going hunting." He picked up his bow and arrows. Perhaps, he thought, I will find my mother. He always looked for his mother when he left the cave.

"Saka, do you have your blue stone?" his grandmother asked.

"Oh-oh! I forgot," said Sakarakaamche, searching through his belongings until he found the precious stone.

"You must remember what your grandfather, Nya, has said and keep your blue stone with you always. Do not go beyond the big hill, and be home before dark."

He walked along the bank of the creek looking for small animals. He and his grandmother had eaten no meat for several weeks. He picked up some flat pebbles and skipped them across the stream, amazed at the ripples they made each time they hit the water.

When the boy reached the hill that marked the limits of his territory in late afternoon, his stomach made rumbling sounds. Then he remembered to look for food. Suddenly, a very large quail appeared. Sakarakaamche aimed his arrow and it hit her in the leg.

"Oh-ow-ow! Do not hurt me anymore," Ahoma cried. The boy was surprised to hear a quail speak and hurried to-ward her. "My leg is broken," she said. "Fix it and I will tell you about your mother." Sakarakaamche gently rubbed her leg and her breast, and Ahoma stood and began to walk.

"One day your mother was gathering grasses and seeds on the other side of the hill," Ahoma said, "and she was seen by Ahsa, the largest and oldest monster eagle in the land. Unfortunately, your mother had left her magic white stone at home, and Ahsa's children were very hungry. The huge eagle swept down, picked up your mother, carried her off to the high mountain, and fed her to his children."

"Where can I find my enemy, the monster eagle?" the boy asked his new friend, the quail.

"Return to this place early in the morning," Ahoma said, "and I will take you to Gwi, your father the Cloud. He will tell you what you must do."

Sakarakaamche walked slowly home. He did not want his grandmother to see his sadness and the tears. When she called him to dinner, he said he was not hungry. He could not yet tell his grandmother the terrible news about his mother.

Very early the next morning Sakarakaamche left the cave without waking his grandmother. His grandfather, Nya, was still on the other side of the mountain and it was too dark to see his father, Gwi. He took with him his bow and arrows and the blue stone.

Two long nights later, Sakarakaamche returned. He no longer ignored his grandmother. "I have much to tell you," he said, "but I am very hungry, and your rat stew and mesquite bread smell so good. If I do not eat right now, I shall certainly drop dead from hunger." Kamalapukwia knew then that everything was all right.

When his stomach was full, Sakarakaamche told his grandmother how he had met Ahoma and about the terrible fate of his poor mother. The boy described how he had found his father on the other side of the hill and related all that Gwi had told him to do.

"I wandered through the grassy fields for many hours," he said. "In the late afternoon when I became very tired, I heard a great noise over me. At first I thought it was my Uncle Thunder, but—to my horror—it was Ahsa! For just a moment I forgot that I was in no danger. My father had told me exactly what would happen. Ahsa picked me up—not very gently—and carried me up to his nest on a crag on the highest mountain.

"He dropped me in front of his family of little eaglets—they were not very little—and they looked at me hungrily. I said to them in my bravest voice, 'Do not hurt me. I am your brother.' I then demanded that they tell me where their parents would sit when they came home, and after I threatened to throw them over the bluff, they told me. I crept quietly to a hidden spot near the place where the two monster parents would sit, and I waited until they came home. Then I killed them, just as Gwi told me to do, with my powerful little blue stone."

The Red Rock Country

3
The Sun People

Sakarakaamche sat on the river bank where he had played as a child watching his mother and grandmother create bowls and cooking pots from the red clay. He had once tried to make a pot himself, but his little fingers were too clumsy. Now the young man sat by the river as Nya had ordered and waited for something to happen.

As Sakarakaamche had grown older and bigger and stronger, he often went past the large hill, and away from the safe canyon. He trekked through the high pine forests to the highest mountain top where he hunted deer, antelope or mountain sheep. Sakarakaamche was very brave; he was also very strong. After wrestling with the wolf, the bear and other fierce animals a few times, they avoided him.

He often met his father, Gwi, on the other side of the hill, and from him Sakarakaamche learned many things. Gwi taught him to hunt only when it was necessary and how to use every part of the dead animal. Nya, his grandfather, gave him wisdom, strength and other powers that the young man did not understand.

"How can I be the father of many people by just sitting on this peaceful bank?" he asked himself? "How can I find a wife just sitting here skipping stones and playing in the clay like a small child? How can I have sons and daughters with-

out a wife? How can I have a wife when my old grandmother is the first woman and only woman in the land?
What can Nya be thinking of?"

The young man picked up a large piece of red clay and
rolled it around in his powerful hands. He rolled it some
more, pressed it and twisted it. To his surprise he soon
made a figure of a woman who looked much like his mother
as he remembered her. Pleased with his efforts, he continued
to roll, twist, punch and pound large globs of clay until he
had made several figures. They look so alive, he thought. If
they were real persons, my grandmother and I would no
longer be lonely. He closed his eyes and dreamed of a canyon full of friends and family.

The young man did not know how long he had
dreamed, but when he awoke and opened his eyes, the figures appeared to be leaving, some alone and some in pairs.
Others were walking toward him. He rubbed his eyes and
looked again. He was not dreaming. Real people had come
to live in the canyon.

Kamalapukwia (First Woman) taught the young women
to gather the fruits, seeds and grasses of the forest and the
desert and to prepare many foods—especially mescal, the
Yavapais' staple food for many centuries. They learned to
gather reeds by the streams for making beautiful and useful
baskets—small baskets, large baskets for storing seeds and
dried berries, waterproof baskets, and very large baskets
that were light and strong enough to carry heavy items a
long distance.

Sakarakaamche (Lofty Wanderer) traveled throughout
the land teaching the Sun People many things that he had
learned from his grandmother, Nya, and Gwi. Once a year
Lofty Wanderer called his people together in the canyon
where he was born. At this time he told them how to live
and play and worship.

The Children of the Sun grew quickly in numbers, and soon their villages were scattered throughout the land. They were happy people, as happy as people could be. They were very healthy from eating the proper foods prepared in the way that First Woman had taught and always working and playing and worshiping in the fresh air. They were never idle but traveled from place to place gathering and hunting, often as many as twenty miles in one day. They lived in caves or temporary homes made from tree branches and animal skins.

The time of the year had come for the people to come together and celebrate their good life. They met near the cave where their common ancestor, Lofty Wanderer, had been born. The summer harvests had been good, and plenty of food had been stored away in their winter homes. They came together to dance and sing and pray—to celebrate their thankfulness as Lofty Wanderer had taught them.

The children were off by themselves playing the games Lofty Wanderer had taught their ancestors. When they grew tired of playing the same old games, two of the older boys decided to make up a new one. They decided to play a war game. But first they made little bows from reeds and arrows tipped with thorns instead of pointed rocks so they could not kill each other.

Then the little boys took sides for battle. For about an hour the children played happily at their new game. No one was able to hit anyone else, and there were no injuries. The children laughed and shouted at one another as they would at any game.

Then one boy got carried away; and imagining himself to be a great warrior, he aimed his arrow directly at his enemy cousin. The arrow hit the target's little brother smack in the middle of his cheek, and the thorn stayed there. The victim became a small child again and began to howl. His older brother, became so angry that he rushed into the enemy territory and started hitting the foe with his bow, using it as a club. The other boys on both sides became excited and entered into the fray.

The little girls who were watching the game became very frightened, and they ran to their mothers crying. The mothers became alarmed and sent the fathers to investigate.

It did not take long for the fathers to break up the battle. Then they went into conference. Unfortunately, the fathers behaved as fathers often do, and each blamed the other man's son for all that had happened. These grown men, who had been friends all their lives, soon became so angry that they started hitting one another.

Suddenly, Lofty Wanderer appeared before his people. "It is now time for the clans to separate," he said. He sent the people who were to become the Yumas to the banks of the Lower Colorado River and the Mohaves farther up the river. The Hualapais moved north to the thick pines and the Havasupais to the Grand Canyon. The Maricopas became tired of always moving around and settled in villages along the Gila River next to the Pimas. Only the Yavapais, the People of the Sun, remained in the land they had always known—in the center of the world where everything had begun.

4

Delche, Paramucca and the Tortilla Flat Treaty
January 1864

Before I can continue my own story I must tell you the story of my people before I was born and how all their troubles began. I must also tell you about Delche, my people's bravest chief.

For hundreds of years, my people, the Yavapai, roamed freely throughout the mountains and river valleys of Central Arizona. I am a Kwoyokopaya, or South Eastern Yavapai. My band of Yavapais made their homes along the Agua Fria, the Verde, and the Salt Rivers and their tributaries. Until the white men came, they moved often searching for the best hunting and gathering areas. There were no cities, ranches or army posts in our country.

In 1863, about two years before I was born, white men found gold on the Hassayampa River near where Prescott is now. In just a few months, hundreds of white men moved into our country. They built army posts, ranches and towns on the land that belonged to my people. One prospector named Paulino Weaver, who was part Indian himself, was a good friend of all Indians. He did not want the Indians and white men to start shooting one another. Weaver made a treaty with Chiefs Chalipun, Paramucca, Delche and others whose names I never learned. At this meeting the chiefs agreed upon a password. Each peaceful Indian would greet each white man he met with "Paulino—tobac—Paulino—tobac." The password did not get around to all the Indians or whites, and peace did not last.

A white man named King Woolsey owned a big ranch on the Agua Fria River. One day unknown Indians rode off toward the east with animals from King Woolsey's ranch. Woolsey organized a party of twenty-eight prospectors and ranchers who went off with their guns toward the Verde River to punish the thieves. They were soon joined by four-teen mounted Maricopa warriors carrying guns that the white men had given them. The Maricopas lived with the Pimas on the Gila River. They were enemies of my people, who in those days had no guns or horses.

Meanwhile, a Yavapai hunting party had been out sev-eral days without seeing any deer. As they were returning to their village overlooking Fish Creek, not far from my fam-ily's village, they came upon Woolsey's party in the Black Canyon and tracked it several miles to the lower Verde Valley.

A few miles north of where the Verde joins the Salt, Mahtla headed for home. Scouting ahead of the others, he had seen Maricopas with the white men. Mahtla ran all the way to tell Paramucca that an enemy war party was headed toward the Salt River Canyon. Chief Paramucca sent out a smoke signal to warn the Yavapais in other villages that white men and Maricopas were coming. Delche came to Paramucca's village for a talk.

Mahtla and Paramucca wanted to line up all their war-riors to show how strong they were. They could assemble more than three hundred men.

"If we fight them we may win, but many Indians will die," Delche said. "Many white men will also die, but some will go back to the army post, and more white men will come to fight us. I think we should get out of here."

Paramucca said, "All our men will line up, and we will hold up a white flag of peace. Then no Indians or white men will die."

King Woolsey and his band set up their camp just south of the Salt River Canyon at a place called Tortilla Flat. Woolsey sent Tonto Jack, a Yuma Indian who had been a captive of the Yavapais for many years, to talk to the chiefs. "The white men want to be your friends," Tonto Jack said. "White chief says if you lay down your arms and go to their camp, he will give you a paper that says to all white men that all Indians are good people and should be treated as friends. When you come to the white man's camp, he will give you pinole and tobacco."

"We are all friends of the white men and do not wish to fight with them," Paramucca replied.

Delche scrambled to a rocky point and shouted, "It is foolish to believe that white men come to our country to make a treaty of friendship. The white men come with Maricopas. The Maricopas have always been our enemy. No Yavapai going to this meeting will live!"

"We will make a peace that will last a long time," Paramucca replied, and unarmed he started down the cliff.

"This is indeed treachery," cried Delche who remained standing on the high cliff overlooking the valley below. "For me and my men—where we stand is close enough."

But thirty-five braves, including his own young son, wanting the taste of tobacco, paid no attention to Delche and joined Paramucca. All except Mahtla, who carried a lance, went unarmed.

When the Indians reached Woolsey's camp, the sun was high in the sky. It was a chilly day, and the campfire was still blazing. With Tonto Jack's help Woolsey directed the Yavapais to sit close to the fire and gave Paramucca a blanket to sit upon. He placed Chief Juan Chivaria and his Maricopa warriors to his left and the white men to his right. Woolsey then whispered something to the men closest to him and passed around the pinole, which was eaten in silence. After the tobacco and sheets of rice paper were passed out, Paramucca began to speak, "My people and I want a peace treaty with the white men that will not be broken. We want to be able to go to the best hunting and gathering places without the fear of being shot down by the white men's guns."

"This is the white man's land now," Woolsey interrupted. "All the gold, the deer, the farm land belong to us. The Indians may kill deer for meat and moccasins, but if you steal the white man's animals, we will kill all your people. Two weeks ago, Apaches stole stock from my ranch on the Agua Fria. You and your people must be punished for these bad acts."

Paramucca became very frightened, but he spoke up to defend his people. "White men say all Indians are Apaches and all Apaches are bad. That is not true. There are some good Apaches, like two men in my village married to Yavapai women. I am a Yavapai, not Apache. My people are Yavapai. They are good Indians who never kill white people. Most never saw a white man before today. Only once we took five ponies and four cattle from the Pimas on the Gila, because we had no meat for three months. Our women and little babies are very hungry. White men punish good Indians for what bad Indians do—just because they are Indians. I think maybe most white men are good, but some are bad."

While Tonto Jack translated, Woolsey touched his hat with his left hand, and the Maricopas and the white men came closer to the Yavapai.

"Paramucca," said Woolsey, "I don't believe what you have said about not killing Americans and stealing our cattle. I know that Apaches stole my animals, and I cannot tell an Apache from any other Indian, and we cannot tell a bad Apache from a good one." Without further warning, Woolsey fired his pistol, and Paramucca was dead. The white men and Maricopas fired their rifles as they approached the Yavapais and the two Apaches who still sat on the cold ground. As the bleeding and injured Indians tried to rise, the enemy fired at them with their pistols. Mahtla, wounded in his left shoulder, pretended he was dead, and at the first opportunity thrust his lance through a young white man's body. Mahtla was unable to remove his lance quickly enough to defend himself, and Woolsey quickly shot him.

Cyrus Lennan the fifteen-year-old brother of Amni White, the agent to the Pimas and Maricopas, was the only white man killed. Paramucca and thirty-four of his braves lay dead. Leaving the massacred Indians in pools of blood, the white men and Maricopas headed back toward their horses and rode away.

One young man lived to tell all that the white men and Maricopas had done to his people. When the shooting began, Waj-ga-thy-match-ju was sitting very still upon a small rock. A bullet hit his shoulder and knocked him to the ground. He lay there unnoticed behind the rock. After the white men left the bloody scene, he quietly crawled away and hid under a bush. He lay there as if he were dead until he was certain that all the white men and the Maricopas were far away. With great difficulty he found his way back to camp in the darkness. The wound was very painful, and he was saddened at the loss of his companions. Wajgathymatchju was also thankful. The blow from the bullet had saved his life.

Wajgathymatchju found Paramucca's camp deserted, and all the huts and belongings of the dead destroyed by burning—as was the custom of his people. It was nearly daylight when he came upon his family at a new camp farther up the mountain. His mother was surprised and happy to see him as she had heard that all the Indians who had gone to Tortilla Flat to talk to the white men had died. "The men from all the villages have joined Delche," she said. "They chose him to be their war leader." Because of Delche, many men in my tribe were still alive.

Cliffs Overlooking Tortilla Flat

5
Delche: McDowell to Reno
September 1865 — January 1870

For many months after the massacre at Tortilla Flat, the bands of Delche and Nanni-Chaddi hid out where the United States Army and its Indian allies—the Pimas and the Maricopas—could not find them. Nanni-Chaddi's band stayed hidden in the Salt River Canyon and Delche's was somewhere in the Mazatzal Mountains.

Then in September 1865, when I was a little baby, the soldiers built an army post called Fort McDowell to protect white settlers from Indians living near there. My people were in real trouble after that. When the soldiers were busy building quarters and mess halls and a hospital, the Pimas went out looking for Yavapais. The Pimas were armed with the white men's guns, but they most often did their killing with clubs. The Pimas usually attacked my people when they were away from their homes gathering foods, and they always attacked before dawn while everyone was asleep. Then they killed all the grown people, burned down their huts and kidnapped the little children. My people were afraid to leave the safety of their mountain and canyon villages. Hunting and gathering became dangerous occupations, and my people were hungry.

Sometimes the troops and the Pimas scouted together. The white men never knew which tribe they attacked or if anybody in that tribe was guilty of any crime. The white men called all Indians Apaches. Some called the Kwoyokopaya, Apache-Mohaves. But my people are not Apaches or Mohaves; we are Yavapais.

In October 1866 Delche and other Yavapai and Apache chiefs went to a meeting at Camp Grant. Captain Guido Ilges, the post commander, agreed to furnish rations and to allow them to make hunting and food gathering expeditions to supplement the rations. The chiefs agreed to settle their people peacefully on a reservation nearby.

But Ilges' boss, General McDowell, said that army officers could not make treaties with Indians, that Indians off the reservation were hostile, and he did not approve the agreement. Later the Indians accepted an agreement drawn up by Colonel Crittendom, and General McDowell approved it. As it turned out, the government did not give the Indians enough food; but when the starving people went off to hunt or gather food, they were shot down on sight.

Some Yavapais and Apaches remained around Camp Grant, but Chief Delche and his warriors went to Fort McDowell promising to be peaceful. Delche asked for rations for his starving people and for protection from the Pimas who were killing them for no reason at all. Delche offered to bring in three hundred more warriors to join Fort McDowell in an attack on Fort Grant. Delche, at this time, did not know that troops from the different posts belonged to the same army.

At that time the post commander, Captain George Sanford, was away from the post so there could be no meeting. When Delche's scouts reported that the Pimas were about to attack the Yavapai camp, the chief did not wait around for Sanford's return. He and his warriors headed for the Mazatzals. If the Yavapais had remained at

McDowell, the post commander could have done little for them. No reservation had been set aside for them near the post, and the troops had barely enough rations to feed themselves.

About a year later, Delche tried again to make peace. He sent messengers to Fort McDowell asking for a reservation where their people could grow crops, hunt and gather, and be safe from their enemies. Delche's people were starving, and they were tired of being blamed for murdering travelers, stealing stock and every bad thing that happened in Arizona. General McDowell told Captain Sanford to choose a good place for a reservation in the Tonto Basin, away from unfriendly Indians and whites and to build Camp Reno there. Sanford decided to locate the new post west of Tonto Creek and south of Mount Ord, and he ordered Lieutenant Richard DuBois to take two infantry companies and construct a wagon road to Camp Reno.

Delche always had scouts keeping an eye on the road building and on the Pimas scouting out of McDowell. When Lieutenant DuBois set up a temporary post called Camp Miller about twenty miles from the post, Delche's scouts sent out smoke signals. Delche then sent a messenger with a flag of truce to ask DuBois for a meeting. Lieutenant DuBois, who had talked to my people when they came to McDowell, understood and spoke many words of our language. He agreed to talk peace if Delche and other members of the tribe would come to him in four days. The messenger agreed.

Four days later, the emissary returned with two young braves. Delche and the others did not come as promised because his scouts had seen Pimas scouting nearby. As DuBois and Delche's messengers talked, nearly sixty Pimas raced over the hill and right into the camp. They surprised and attacked the Yavapais and wounded two of them.

Lieutenant DuBois acted quickly. He pointed his pistol at the Pimas and frightened them away.

Two days later, the wounded messengers were well enough to return to Delche's camp in the Mazatzal Mountains where they told of the brave young white officer who had saved them from death by their ancient enemies. DuBois sent word to the Pima agent and the Fort McDowell commander to keep the Pima scouts away from his camp.

Several weeks later, Delche and fifty warriors came to Camp Miller asking for protection from the Pimas and the Maricopas. Lieutenant DuBois proposed that Delche's people settle on Tonto Creek where they would be free to hunt and gather. He also agreed to give them rations, clothing, and blankets, but he would not give them guns and bullets. He said that when they became peaceful farmers, they could ask for anything. Delche and DuBois soon became great friends.

When the meeting was over, most of the Indians returned to their villages, but Delche and eight men remained at Camp Miller for another day. The chief invited the lieutenant to visit his village, and DuBois agreed to go alone and unarmed. DuBois was very brave. He was the first white military man to visit Delche's camp—and I think the only one. After talking for several hours around a campfire in the Mazatzal Mountains, Delche's warriors agreed to settle in the Tonto Basin where they could be safe from the Pimas and Maricopas and where they could become peaceful farmers. The next morning, eight warriors escorted DuBois back to his camp.

Several days later, Delche and about seventy warriors arrived to stay at Camp Miller. When DuBois and his men moved and established a new camp called Camp Carroll, Delche and his band settled nearby. This time women and children came with them..

In February 1868, Delche's good white friend, Lieutenant DuBois, left for the East. Delche could not understand
why the soldiers kept changing chiefs. Lieutenant George
Chilson who replaced DuBois kept up the friendship with
the Indians. Delche and his people continued to camp near
Camp Carroll.

After Major David Clendinen, the commander of Fort
McDowell, talked to Delche, he believed the Indians to be
peaceful and willing to work, and he gave them seeds. The
next day the Indians began to work their fields near Tonto
Creek.

In April 1868 while Delche and several warriors visited
Camp Carroll, Major Andrew Alexander, the new commander of Fort McDowell, rode into camp. Alexander was
angry. The troops had traveled over two hundred miles
looking for the Indians who had stolen cattle near Tucson,
and they found neither the missing animals nor the thieves.

Major Alexander's interpreter told Delche to remain in
camp because Alexander wanted to talk to him. The chief
agreed to the meeting. However, while the major talked to
Lieutenant Chilson, Delche's scouts spied cavalry troops
and Pima scouts heading toward the camp. Delche and his
band bolted for the mountains. Alexander became angrier
and ordered his men to run down Delche and his warriors.

The Yavapais ran into the hills and were soon out of
sight of the cavalry and the Pimas. When the troops were
near his hiding place, Delche rose up alone on a high pro-
jecting rock. He pointed a rifle at the troops and shouted,
"Captain DuBois is a good man. He always kept his promises to me. Captain Alexander is no friend to my people. My
people are now at war with the United States."

As Major Alexander's troops began to shoot at him,
Delche scampered down the opposite side of the cliff. The
soldiers were in quick pursuit, but they found no sign of
Delche or his men.

Delche decided not to go to war after all. When Chilson and his men reached the site for Camp Reno, Delche's people built huts near the soldiers' tents.

I do not remember being at Camp Reno in the days when I was a very small child; but a few days after I was captured, Company G camped there in the ruins. About thirty years later, I visited this beautiful place where my people wanted to live forever. A large variety of hardwood trees and plenty of grass for the stock grow in the meadow where the post was built, and cool fresh water trickles down from the high mountains where tall pine trees grow.

The Yavapais continued to work in their fields near Tonto Creek. They soon harvested a good crop of corn and beans. Luckily for Delche, Alexander's troops were kept busy chasing down Indians who constantly attacked the mail parties and raided the corrals of white settlers and Pimas.

A great mystery surrounded Delche. Many soldiers and settlers blamed Delche's band for attacks on herds and wagon trains near McDowell, as far west as Wickenburg and La Paz, and as far south as Picacho. How could these Indians have been in so many places and at the same time be working their fields or cutting and bundling grass that they exchanged to the quarter master for extra rations?

Delche's luck did not last. One day while he was enjoying a friendly visit with Lieutenant Chilson, the post doctor called Delche to the hospital tent. "Good day," said Delche as he approached the doctor. The doctor replied by pointing his rifle at the chief and firing. Immediately, Delche who was wounded in the chest turned away from his assailant and walked away with his head held high. His warriors followed in the same manner as everyone in the camp remained silent. Not a word was said by the white men or Indians until Delche was outside the fort. Then Delche shrieked one horrible war cry; and almost instantly he and his men disappeared into the rocky hills.

A few weeks later, unknown Indians attacked Camp
Reno. They ran off all the stock and set fire to all the buildings. No soldiers were harmed. Fort Reno was soon abandoned.

The Author at the Site of Old Camp Reno

6
The Peace Talk
September 1871

I always looked forward to an adventure away from my home, and I felt very excited—and just a little bit scared—as I led my old grandfather out of the Salt River Canyon. Several hundred Indians from the Mazatzal Mountains and the Tonto Basin, including the tribe of Nanni-Chaddi—the tribe that I belonged to—were on their way to Fort McDowell to talk peace with the United States Government. I was still a small boy and my grandfather was nearly blind. We could not keep up with the others, but grandfather knew the way well and used my eyes to keep us on the trail. The old man warned me to always look and listen for signs of the enemy.

At this time I was too young to understand what was happening. Years later, I learned that some white men in the East were friends of the Indians. They wanted the government to make peace with the Indians. So President Ulysses Grant sent Mr. Vincent Colyer of the Peace Commission to talk to all the hostile Indians of Arizona—that is all the Indians but the Pimas and Maricopas and Papagos who joined the white soldiers against other tribes.

In September 1871, Mr. Colyer came to Fort McDowell hoping to meet with Indians from the many bands living near the Salt River and Tonto Creek. He wanted to end the fighting and put my people on reservations where our enemies could not hurt us and where we would never be hungry. The government would give us all the food we needed. Mr. Colyer was a good friend of the Indians.

Mr. Colyer especially wanted to meet Delche, the most important chief of my people. The soldiers sent up smoke signals, and a scouting party carrying white flags went out looking for Delche. But they could not find the chief or other members of his band. Delche had not visited Fort McDowell since he had been shot by a doctor—for no reason at all—a year earlier at Camp Reno. However, two days after Mr. Colyer left for Camp Verde, messengers from Delche went to Fort McDowell asking for peace. Soon Delche and other chiefs and warriors from many Yavapai bands began to assemble at Fort McDowell for a meeting with Major Dudley, the post commander.

Grandfather and I traveled all day. Finally, we arrived at a quiet place surrounded by thick chaparral and overlooking a small stream. Grandfather said, "This is a good, safe place to camp for the night. We will stop here."

I felt very hungry and my stomach growled. We had brought no food with us, and we had not eaten all day. The big dog that traveled with us had at other times caught small game and, once, a young deer, but on this trip the dog had killed nothing. I was eager to reach Fort McDowell. The soldiers had promised food to all the Indians who came to the post.

My grandfather said, "Go quickly. Find us some wood." I always obeyed my grandfather. While I was gone, the old man killed the dog and skinned it.

When I returned with the wood, I recognized the dead animal as my former companion, but I said nothing. I helped Grandfather dig a hole and watched as he made a fire with the wood and covered it with stones. When the fire had burned down to the level of the hole, the old man laid the meat on the hot stones and covered it with grass, brush, and earth so that no steam could escape. The roast cooked all night. In the morning when we uncovered it, the meat smelled so good. For a change, grandfather and I had all we wanted to eat, and there was enough to last until we reached our people's camp across the river from Fort McDowell. I was very hungry, and the dog meat tasted as good as any other.

Over two hundred Indians from four different bands— Chalipun's from Green Valley, Nanni-Chaddi's from the Salt River Canyon, Ascavotil's from the Four Peaks area and Delche's from the Mazatzals—camped across the river from McDowell. They were mostly young warriors, but there were a few other small boys to play with. In the evening Grandfather and another old man entertained us with stories about other times.

Indian chiefs and soldiers in blue uniforms assembled on the parade ground. Soldiers gave blankets and rations to the chiefs. I later learned that Delche made a long speech. The chief said that his people were tired of hiding from the white men. He promised peace forever if we could live in our own country in the Tonto Basin where our people could hunt deer and gather summer fruits; plant corn, beans, melons and pumpkins; and be safe from unfriendly Indians and white men. Delche said that God made Indians and white men, and his people had as much right to the land as the white men. Delche asked for a paper with all the promises written on it. He said he would put a rock upon the paper. The treaty would be good until the rock melted. He said if the white men did not keep their promises, he would put the paper in a hole and cover it with dirt.

Chalipun, Nanni-Chaddi and Ascovotil did not make speeches. They agreed with all that Delche said. Their people wanted to live in the Tonto Basin and become peaceful farmers. Major Dudley and the other army officers also agreed, but because army officers cannot make treaties Major Dudley promised to send off a written treaty for President Grant to sign.

When the council ended, the Indians collected wood from the post wood pile, built fires and began to cook their beef. Just as I had eaten my first mouthful of meat, my father came to me and said, "One of Delche's scouts has learned that Pimas are coming. Hurry to the mountains!" I snatched as much cooked meat as I could, grabbed my grandfather's arm and fled silently from the camp. We feared the Pimas who had guns and horses and always attacked our camps when they found us.

The old people and the children went first before the sun went down. As others followed, the young warriors kept singing and beating the drums very loudly so the soldiers did not notice anyone leaving the camp. By midnight, Pah-gin-yan-ga (Dried Up) and about six other young men were the only Indians left in the camp. They crept up toward the stable on their hands and knees, keeping their eyes on the guard who was walking toward them. When the soldier turned to walk the other way, the warriors dashed up to the stable, and they came out unnoticed with all the horses. As they crossed the river, the horses protested loudly and alarmed the soldiers' camp. Soldiers fired shots at the escaping Indians and horses, but they hit nothing.

All night long, the warriors drove the horses over the hills and mountains until they reached the place where my people camped. The horses were soon killed and cut up into steaks. The next morning we looked back and saw soldiers coming across the valley. Two warriors held up the meat for the soldiers to see. The soldiers fired a few shots but stayed in the foothills. That night we filled our stomachs with horse meat.

Yavapai Warrior in Traditional Clothing Holding Club
Photographer unknown

7
Terror in the Desert
Summer 1872

I remember well that terrible day when soldiers killed my mother, and I had to care for two children—a little brother and a little sister. I remember the incident as if it happened just a few days ago.

In those days, the women in our tribe traveled long distances to many different places to gather wild fruits and seeds. The young men hunted deer and hardly ever came back without one. Deer meat was our most important food. Although we were often hungry, we had more things to eat than we do now. We did not have to buy anything to prepare a meal

In midsummer, my family went to the rolling hills near Fort McDowell so the women could gather the ripe desert fruits. My father and uncle were always on guard against white men and unfriendly Indians. The women picked the saguaro fruits with a stick made of two long saguaro ribs tied together with a wooden hook at the end. The family ate the fresh fruits as fast as the women picked them. Every seed was saved and dried for later use.

My little brother was about three years old, and my baby sister who was only a few months old demanded many feedings at my mother's breast. Mother always found time to smile lovingly at me. My aunt had five children, and the older ones helped look after the younger ones. After spending two days in the hot sun, the women had filled several baskets with seeds. They were very happy with their efforts. They were also very tired and wanted to return to the safety of their village in the Salt River Canyon.

My father, Mee-kee-et-ah-ee-ta (Standing Squirrel), was also anxious about his family's safety. "Head toward home," he said. "I will go ahead to make certain our trail is safe from soldiers. Last night I had a very bad dream, and it may be dangerous to go that way. In my dream I saw men in blue clothing riding great horses across a great river of red water. I fear that the soldiers might watch the trail leading to our canyon." Father was thinking of the place—named Tortilla Flat by the white men and called Bloody Tanks by the Yavapais—where nine years earlier white men had deceived and killed so many of our people and where he feared they might kill again. "I will go ahead and watch for enemies. I will call out if there is any danger, and you can run for safety." My father left us and soon was over the hill and out of sight.

My mother led the way to the top of the hill and nearly stepped on a large bluish lizard lying on its back with blood dripping from its mouth. "I fear," she said, "that this is a sign that something bad will happen to one of us."

"Perhaps we should not go to the bottom lands," Uncle Mee-sa-kau-wa (Egg Foot because of a bunion) said. "You wait here. I will run ahead and talk the situation over with Meekee."

About fifteen minutes later, my uncle returned. "There was no sign of Meekee," he said, "we shall continue this way."

At the bottom of the hill not far from the Verde River, my mother noticed that the mesquite beans were ripe and ready for picking. The beans, the seeds from the saguaro fruits, and the nuts that she would gather in the fall would be ground into a coarse flour, stored in baskets sealed with plant gum, and used in making bread. She would need many seeds and nuts to provide enough bread for her family during the long winter.

My mother placed my little brother, the baby and me in a shady spot under some large trees. "You wait here," she said to me. "There can be no danger, or your father would have called to us." She had forgotten the dream and the lizard. She removed the large burden basket from her back. It held most of the family's belongings and the seeds she had harvested. She carried a smaller basket to hold the seeds she planned to gather. "I will be gone only a few minutes," she said. "Perhaps your father will kill a deer. Then we can find a safe place to camp and have a fine feast." She called to my aunt and uncle and to my grandparents, but they were moving slowly, and she went on without them.

A few minutes later, the rest of the family arrived at the shady spot and after a brief rest prepared to follow my mother. Then I heard my father's warning yell from beyond the curve of the stream. The warning was followed by a very loud bang, then another and another, and finally by my mother's awful scream. I knew that something terrible had happened to her.

"Those loud noises were from white men's guns. I fear your mother has been shot," said my uncle sadly. My aunt began to cry softly. I thought I would never be happy again. But I could not cry.

"We must turn back," my uncle said. We are in great danger. "Thya, quickly take the little ones to that gulch over there. It is narrow and steep so be careful. When I get the others to safety, I will return for you."

I was only a small boy, about seven, but I led my little brother by the hand and carried the baby on my back in her cradle board. We hid behind dense creosote bushes, but we could hear the terrible noise from the soldiers' weapons. I was so frightened that I had difficulty breathing. We crawled deeper into the thick brush where I finally felt safe from any enemy and could breathe easily.

It was dark when my uncle returned for us. As we reached the top of the hill, I saw my father coming toward us. His eyes were red from crying, and my grandparents and aunt and uncle began to cry. "Hoomothya, your mother must have died at the first few shots. I was high up in the hills, and it was too late to save her, but I tried to warn you," he said putting his arm around me. My little brother and sister were sound asleep.

My father continued, "The soldiers must have heard me too. They soon headed in my direction. I climbed even higher until I reached the top of a high, steep, rocky hill, at a safe distance above them. I defended myself by shooting arrows at them and hurling down large boulders." Father paused and wiped a tear from his cheek with his finger. "Three horses were knocked down, and the others bolted down the canyon without their riders. I saw soldiers pulling arrows from their backs, and I heard them cry out as they did so."

Before dawn when my father and uncle went to search for my mother's body, my father said, "You must leave immediately for our village. Stay in high country and watch out for soldiers." He paused and looked at me. "Thya, take your brother and sister. If there is great danger and you cannot take them, run and save your life." Then my father said sadly, "You need not take the baby as there is no milk for her now."

Suddenly, my aunt stopped crying. "I will take my sister's child," she said. "I have milk for her." She had a child about a month older.

My father and uncle caught up with us about noon. They had found my mother's body and burned it with all the things that belonged to her. It was the custom of my people to cremate their dead.

We hurried on our way to reach our canyon homes where no enemy—white soldiers or Pimas—could surprise us. We carefully avoided the main trails and reached Fish Creek Canyon before dark. We descended the canyon for some distance, then climbed the hills to the mesa beyond the creek and then to our home overlooking the Salt River.

Steep Walls of the Salt River Canyon

8
Raiding the Corrals
of the Enemy
Autumn 1872

After my mother's death, my family stayed in our village where we felt protected from a surprise attack. Only my father left the safety of the canyon and joined other men from nearby villages on raids to obtain food for their families. Most Yavapai bands nearly starved to death when soldiers shut off the food supply. Our band, the band of Nanni-Chaddi, unlike many others, had stored a large supply of seeds, nuts, and berries away in our winter cave homes. But meat was scarce. The men dared not go to the usual hunting places because well-armed white men shot Indians on sight. They felt much safer running off animals from the corrals of the enemy. Since the arrival of white men in our country, we had learned to like horse meat.

My people had always feared and hated the Pimas—we thought they were evil spirits—and stealing from them was right. Also, after the soldiers shot my poor mother, my father hated all white men. Killing an enemy or being killed was not nearly as important to him as getting food for his family.

Many men from our tribe, including Delche's three sons, risked their lives to run off horses and mules from the Pima villages and from the white settlers in the Salt River Valley. Chiefs Nanni-Chaddi and Delche did not often go on the raids. Delche's son Baw-si-di-yan-a (Round, Thin, Greasy-Looking Mouth) usually led the raiders.

Our village was an important meeting place for many Yavapai bands. After the raiders drove off the enemy's animals, they usually escaped to our canyon, the place that the Pima scouts feared and the white men could not find. The stolen animals were left, hidden in a meadow two miles away from our cave homes. Only mountain sheep and my people could climb the dangerous canyon wall. The animals to be immediately cooked and eaten were cut up and carried on the warriors' backs up the steep trail to their cave homes. Once as I watched a man try to force a mule over this trail, the animal fell over the wall and disappeared.

Much of the time, especially since the death of my mother, I did not know where my father was. I looked forward to his return and hearing about his many adventures. Once, after his party had raided a settlement in Phoenix, Mexican and American civilians chased the raiding party to Camelback Mountain. My father saved the day by climbing quickly to the top of a steep and rocky cliff, holding down his bow, and helping the others up the cliff and to safety.

Late in October, my father brought a mule for the family to eat. I was hungry for meat, but visitors seeking shelter in the Salt River caves arrived at meal time, and the portions were small.

My father said to his brother-in-law, "Another mule grazes in the meadow below. Kill it when you need meat. Please look after my children. I am going near the mouth of the river on another raid and will be gone for about five days."

When my father had been out with the raiding party several days beyond the expected time of return, I feared I might never see him again. My uncle also worried and asked the old medicine man to perform a ritual to discover the fate of my father and the others.

Curious like most little boys, I watched as my uncle and another man filled the old medicine man's mouth with sand, tied a cloth firmly around it, and tied his hands behind his back. I had never seen such a ceremony before, and I asked, "How can a man with his mouth full of sand tell us where my father is?"

For two hours, we stood around the man as he lay upon the ground as if dead. "Can a dead man tell us about my father?" I asked myself. Then, suddenly, I began to hear whisper-soft sounds coming from the old man. Slowly, the sounds became louder. I whispered, "The medicine man has come back to life!"

Uncle Meesakauwa untied the man and removed his gag. The medicine man spit out the sand, rinsed his mouth out for several minutes, took a long drink, and began to speak to the anxious spectators slowly and in a very gruff voice. "You need—worry—no more. Your—young men— have met—no enemy," he stammered. "They will return—in two days—with many animals."

Two days later, my father returned from a successful raid. The four horses that grazed in the hidden meadow would provide meat for a long time. My father asked his brother-in-law to move the family farther up the canyon wall to the main village of Nanni-Chaddi. Knowing that his family was safe, he left on another raid.

9

Captured
December 19, 1872

One morning I awoke long before the sun's rays reached the canyon wall. Sunlight never entered the cave home where my family spent the winter. "Eat quickly and come with me," Uncle Meesakauwa said. "We are going on a journey up north to take a horse to my brother." I was still sleepy, but I jumped up from my bed of straw and hastily grabbed a slab of mescal and a hunk of horse meat. I was very quiet so as not to wake the others.

Grandfather was awake. "Take your Navajo blanket and wear some moccasins," the old man said. "There will be snow in the mountains. Take enough mescal and horse meat to last three days. You will not come to another Indian camp before then."

I felt very sad at leaving my grandfather. "Who will lead him around?" I asked myself, "and who will take care of him?" My grandmother had died a few weeks earlier, and the old man would be all alone. I had a frightening feeling that I might never see the dear old man again, and my eyes filled with tears. I did not think about my little brother and sister as my aunt always cared for them with her little ones, nor about my father who was seldom home. I thought I could hear my grandfather's mournful cry until we were several miles from our cave home.

I wore only a breech cloth. I had no moccasins because I was too young to make them for myself. It was very early, and the stars shone brightly in the sky. I rode the horse bareback grabbing its mane with one hand. Shivering from the cold, I kept wrapping the blanket closer to my body with my free hand. My uncle wore a coyote skin shirt, discarded army trousers, and moccasins that came to just below his knees. He carried a bow and a quiver full of arrows over his shoulder and a bundle containing horse meat and mescal on his back.

We continued our journey until almost noon when we came to a little stream and drank the icy water and ate a few morsels of mescal and horse meat. We crossed the creek and followed a sandy wash that led to Fort McDowell. Keeping a safe distance from the post and out of the soldiers' sight, we traveled north to the foot of the mountains.

As the sun disappeared behind the mountains to the west, we left the trail, went for a short distance up a narrow gulch, and camped beside a dying mesquite surrounded by thick brush. My uncle built a fire to burn off the brush. A brisk wind, which increased the chill of the evening air, forced the flames higher than usual. I wrapped my naked little body tightly in my blanket and crouched as close to the fire as possible. When the fire had burned most of the brush, we had a scanty meal of mescal and meat. Uncle Meesakauwa then built another but smaller fire and spread grass on the ground for our beds. "If the fire begins to go out," he yawned, "get up and keep it going by putting on more twigs."

I was very tired. Lying close to the fire, I wrapped the blanket tightly around me, but my uncle snored so loudly I was unable to sleep. I thought that any enemy between us and McDowell could hear him. After we had passed

McDowell, I was bothered by the feeling that someone was following us, but my uncle never looked back. A Yavapai child never questioned his elders. Any enemy within miles surely saw that big fire, I thought, shivering from cold and fear. My people did not build large fires unless they wanted to send a message or were having an important celebration. My uncle continued to snore.

I got up about midnight, put a small bundle of sticks on the fire, lay down, covered my head with my blanket, and within minutes uncovered it. "Did I really hear a sound out there?" I asked myself, "or was I imagining it?" Then I heard a rumbling sound in the gulch. I raised my head in the direction of the sound. I heard men's voices. The voices were getting closer, but I could not understand the words. I jumped up, jerked the blanket from my uncle. "Soldiers or Pimas are coming," I whispered. My uncle woke at once, jumped over a large bush, and was out of sight. I, a small, terrified child, was unable to jump over the bush. I could only crawl under it.

I thought that I would run into the hills. But just then, shots were fired into the campfire, scattering sparks high in the air. I fell to the ground, and although nearly dead with fear, I managed to creep up a hill toward some large rocks —all the while hearing someone close behind me. I crawled into a hole, thinking I would prefer to face snakes or coyotes than Pimas or soldiers. Luckily for me, the owner was not at home.

Someone poked a long stick into the hole in the rocks. It came very close but could not reach me. I shivered in the cold air. Naked except for my breach cloth, because in my escape I forgot the Navajo blanket, I kept turning from side to side in an attempt to keep warm. During the night, the air became even colder, and the freezing winds blew among the rocks. All night long, I heard soldiers and Pimas moving about the large fire that lit up the entrance of my hide-out.

Occasionally, I saw the bare or moccasined foot of an Indian and the heavy boot of a soldier and wondered why the enemy remained near my hiding place. They could not see me and could not know that I was there. I tried to pray to Lofty Wanderer and wished my people still carried the blue or white stones to keep them safe.

As daylight filtered through the bushes, I knew that the sun was high over the distant hills. The thought of being out in the sunlight made me shiver uncontrollably, and my teeth clattered. I felt colder than ever, but not once did I think that I might die. I thought only of escape. There was more activity by the soldiers and their scouts, and I thought I heard them mount their horses and leave the camp site. Soon the sounds from the enemy seemed farther and farther away. Finally, I could hear only the birds cheerfully chirping in the morning sunshine.

Eager to leave my tight quarters and find another hiding place, I crawled in the opposite direction from where I had entered, left through another opening, and came out close to a tall tree and a very large rock. I looked around at the great world about me, and for a moment wondered if there were friendly Indians nearby. I was only about seven years old— and I feared the unknown. So I decided to head for my cave home and my people. I was cold and hungry and homesick. I climbed to the top of the rock to get a sense of direction and saw the west side of Four Peaks. Then I turned around and came face to face with a long row of men in blue clothing. Then I knew that they had known all the time I was there and were waiting for me to come out of hiding.

I was too frightened to move, so I stood there—naked, shivering and teeth clattering—facing the enemy. The only time I had seen a white man before was when I had gone with my grandfather to Fort McDowell over a year ago. I had never seen a Pima, but I knew the column of Indians with the painted black faces must be the long dreaded enemy. I knew there was no escape and wondered when they would shoot me—as they had my poor mother.

Suddenly, a soldier, who seemed to be the leader, grabbed me by the arm and pulled me over the rocks and bushes. He did not seem to care whether I got hurt or not. Although I kicked and hit and bit fiercely, he dragged me away like a dog.

A View of Four Peaks in December

Part II

Mike and Captain Burns
with the Fifth Cavalry
1872 — 1875

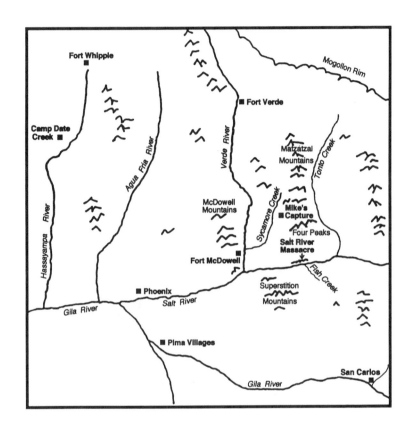

Scouting in Arizona with
the Fifth Cavalry
1872-1875

10
Mike and Captain Burns
December 19 – 28, 1872

I learned later—when I could understand English—that the officer who captured me was Captain James Burns. He first arrived in Arizona with Troop G, 5th Cavalry in 1871. While on scouting duty out of Camp Date Creek, Burns got to know many Yavapais who camped outside the post. He often defended them when he thought other white men treated them unfairly.

Late in November 1872, Captain Burns reported to Fort McDowell to take part in General George Crook's massive campaign against the Indians in the Tonto Basin. A few days later, Captain Burns, Lieutenant Earl Thomas, the men of Company G, Chief Scout Al Sieber, nearly one hundred Pimas and a mule train carrying rations for thirty days set out from Fort McDowell to conquer the enemy—my people.

Burns wondered about the trail made by the moccasin tracks of one Indian—made by my uncle—and one horse—ridden by me. Two hours later, he wondered at the smoke and flames of a large fire near Sugar Loaf Butte. Knowing that Indians normally did not build large fires, Burns feared that that the enemy might be trying to lead him into an ambush. He warned his men to be cautious.

As Captain Burns and his troops approached our campfire about two o'clock in the morning, the Pimas' loud war whoops warned the enemy (my uncle and me). Scouts soon found the tracks of a horse and my uncle's moccasined feet leading into the hills and the prints of my small, bare feet leading into the bushes. Burns sent Sieber and several Pima scouts to search the hills for my uncle.

Burns believed that a young child was hiding somewhere in the rocks and bushes. A scout probed under the rocks and into the bushes with a long stick but found nothing. The soldiers, dressed in trousers, heavy shirts, and gloves and well supplied with blankets, shivered from the cold. A few suffered from frostbitten fingers and toes. Burns, thinking the little Indian could not stay long in his hiding place on such a cold night, decided to wait for me to come out of hiding. For five long hours, he waited for me to appear.

My captor placed me on his horse behind the saddle and handed me a blanket to cover my naked little body. By this time all the solders were on their horses, and Troop G of the Fifth Cavalry headed toward Fort McDowell.

After going some distance, I stopped shivering from the cold and was prepared to face whatever would happen to me. Then suddenly, a small bird flew up in the horse's face. The startled animal became so hard to manage that Captain Burns put me off and made me run ahead of the troops. As I came near the pack train, several Pima and Maricopa scouts with ghastly black-painted faces ran toward me. I was afraid that they would either bash my head in or sell me into slavery. So I began to cry and ran as fast as I could back to the soldiers, begging for someone to take me up on his horse.

Captain Burns took pity on me and lifted me up again on his horse, and we rode into camp, which was on the creek that my uncle and I had crossed the day before. While I was still riding with Burns, the same Pima scouts who had chased me earlier, came right up to us, grabbed hold of my legs and tried to pull me off the horse. I became frightened again and howled like a baby. Burns took out his pistol and shouted at the Pimas until they backed off. I began to think that perhaps this white man was a friend, and I soon realized that he was the leader of all these soldiers and Indian scouts.

I had a bad time getting used to the new and strange food that the officers shared with me. When Lieutenant Thomas gave me a sour pickle, I wrinkled up my face and the officers laughed at me. After a few bites, I liked the sour taste. They also laughed when I scraped the butter, which I thought smelled bad, from the bread. I was still a very small boy and did not enjoy being laughed at. I was too young and too uncivilized to understand their jokes, and I wanted to cry. I just pretended to be a grown up Indian and kept a very stern face.

After the noon meal when the bright sun warmed the air, Captain Burns and Lieutenant Thomas took me to a creek and held me under the cool water. I believed they were going to drown me, and I screamed in terror. But my screams were all for nothing. Burns washed me thoroughly from head to foot with soap. After he had dried me off, he dressed me in a warm shirt and trousers so large they had to be tied on. I was thankful that I was no longer naked. Later, I learned that I smelled very badly and was covered with lice after spending the night in the animal hole.

The next day, the two officers again shared their mid-day meal with me. I knew they were talking about me. I could not understand a word, but I knew by the way these strange white men looked at me and by the softness in their voices that they were saying kind things about me. Later, when I could understand English, Lieutenant Thomas told me about his conversation with Captain Burns.

"I think the boy needs a name," Lieutenant Thomas said. "Let's make him an Irish Indian and call him Mike

Burns." From then on Captain Burns was like a father to me, and I was like his own little boy. That is how I got the name by which I am still known today. Captain Burns was my best friend as long as he lived. Lieutenant Thomas comforted me years later when I was a stranger far away from my own country.

On the third day after my capture, Captain Burns brought two Pima scouts to talk to me. Captain Burns must have told them to remove their war paint so that they would look less frightening, and he probably warned them not to abuse the child who was now the son of a captain. The Pimas and I—a small Yavapai child—could not understand each other, so an interpreter accompanied us to the top of the hill near the Mazatzal Mountains where we could see the whole countryside. One Pima pointed in the direction of my cave home in the Salt River Canyon and said, "ah-oh." An interpreter translated, "Is that where you used to live?"

I answered, "uh," which could mean either yes or no. The Pimas seemed satisfied and we all went back down the hill.

I was glad when that meeting was over. I thought that the Pimas were too afraid of the ghosts in our canyon to lead the soldiers to our village.

The next morning, the command trekked through the foothills of the Mazatzals to the Tonto Basin. We rested until late afternoon and followed a small stream to Tonto Creek where the scouts had seen signs of Indians. The command charged down both sides of the creek to where it joined the Salt.

About the sixth day after my capture, Company G camped near the Superstition Mountains. Here we were joined by six more companies of the Fifth Cavalry from Camp Grant.

I was slowly getting over my first fright of being captured and taken away from the only life I had ever known.

When I saw the great number of Pimas leaving my country and heading toward the Gila River, I feared less for my family. There were many moments when I still missed my grandfather terribly, but I was beginning to enjoy the comforts provided by my new white father. I had more food to eat than I could ever remember and enough clothing to keep me warm.

After dinner on the seventh day, which I know now was Christmas, Captain Burns and Lieutenant Thomas took me to Major William Brown's tent about a mile away. Major Brown commanded all the troops from Camp Grant. When I saw hundreds of soldiers and all the pack animals, guns, and ammunition, I began to realize that the situation was very serious; but it was too much for a seven-year-old boy to understand.

When I saw the many Indian scouts, I began to understand. Some scouts were Apaches who had once been friends of my people. Many were Yavapais from my own tribe who went to live at Camp Grant with the soldiers and had no people. Nanni-Chaddi and Delche did not trust them. The Yavapai scouts knew all the trails and camping places in the Tonto Basin, and they could go through the country no matter how dark the night might be. Others of my family might still be alive today if these scouts had not helped the army.

Major Brown spoke to the officers, soldiers, and scouts. "The orders from General Crook are to destroy Chiefs Delche and Nanni-Chaddi and their warriors."

Major Brown paused and looked sternly at the scouts. "Even if you are related to him, you must track down Chief Delche." Brown turned his eyes in my direction and continued. "Scout Esquinosquizn claims that Delche is hiding out in his village in the Four Peaks Mountains." I shivered as I heard the name of my people's big chief, and when I heard the major's words translated into my language, I knew that something terrible was about to happen.

"Another order," Brown said, "is to wipe out Nanni-Chaddi's village, if it can be found. One of our guides, Nantje, was raised there and may agree to lead us to it." When I heard the final order, tears filled my eyes, and I began to tremble, but I behaved like a grown-up warrior and I did not cry. Nanni-Chaddi was the chief of my family.

I joined the Yavapai scouts for a meeting about my people. Nantje, who was my cousin and the chief Yavapai scout for Major Brown, took me aside and said, "We must tell the soldiers the truth or we shall die. Our people will be hunted down now or later. There is no escape for them."

I told Nantje everything—where I had been, how I had been taken, and how many days had passed since my uncle had escaped and left me all alone to face the enemy. By now, I thought, my uncle must have told my people that I am dead or captured, and they must know they are in danger. They should know that a little boy like me would lead them back to my cave home.

The morning after my talk with Nantje, the two commands followed the south side of the Salt River for about twenty-five miles to Tonto Creek where they set up camp near present-day Roosevelt Dam. Here in the springtime the grass grows green, the trees blossom, and the scent of the wild flowers is so sweet. This was a favorite place for my people, the Kwoyokopaya or Southeastern Yavapai. Game and other foods were plentiful, and the bottom lands are level for camping and growing crops. There is no more such life. All who used to spend happy days there have died or were forced to leave this land. I am the only Indian who lives to tell about how my people lost the land they believed was theirs forever.

Before the sun was up over the hills on the morning of December 27, every man in the camp was ready to march.

Canteens and bundles containing blankets and rations were strapped to their backs and ammunition was strapped around their waists and shoulders. I carried nothing but my blanket and a canteen of water. The command must have been a mile long. Scouts from my people and a captured woman led the way. The soldiers followed them south over the same trail we had traveled the day before. About noon we rested beside a creek bordered with walnut, willow and cottonwood trees.

Late in the afternoon the command began to climb the steep hill above the Salt River Canyon. Halfway to the top, the scouts reached the camp where I had once lived happily with my family. They surrounded and searched the place—but just as I could have told them, if anyone had asked—my family had moved, and the soldiers found nothing.

Nantje said to Major Brown, "Tomorrow, I will lead the troops to Nanni-Chaddi's hide out, but we must go before dawn. If the enemy finds us on this trail, not one of us will come back alive." Nantje was about to lead six companies of the Fifth Cavalry against less than one hundred helpless and innocent Indians—his own people and mine.

That night when I rolled up in my blanket and thought about all that had happened and what I believed was about to happen, I became frightened again. The white men had stolen our lands and destroyed our villages—and my people were here a long time before them They killed my people and shot my poor mother. I shivered, as I remembered how they kept me—a poor little seven-year-old boy—out in the rocks that cold night until I nearly died alone in that dark and freezing hole. It was a miracle I survived. I cried softly and prayed to Lofty Wanderer to save my people.

11

Massacre in the
Salt River Canyon
December 28, 1872

An hour before dawn, all the Fifth Cavalry except the soldiers who stayed behind with the mules began the difficult trek up and down the narrow, rough and winding trail above the Salt River Canyon. With Nantje in the lead, the troops marched quickly in the cold night air toward the summit.

When we reached a ridge overlooking the river, we were ordered to halt and lie flat upon the cold ground so the enemy could not see us. Nantje and the scouts went on ahead. Within minutes they returned to report that just around the bend in the trail, they had come upon several recently abandoned huts. A little farther down the trail, they had found five horses and nine mules grazing in a green meadow. Nantje said that high on a bluff directly above the abandoned huts was the large village of Nanni-Chaddi.

"I have scouted this area often and have never seen signs of a large village," Lieutenant Ross said.

Nantje smiled. "Wait and see," he said. Only I knew for sure that what Nantje said was true. Major Brown trusted Nantje and ordered Lieutenant Ross and fifteen sharpshooters to continue on the trail to Nanni-Chaddi's village.

Nantje told Major Brown that warriors from Nanni-Chaddi's clan often joined warriors from other villages in raids. Major Brown ordered Captain Burns and Company G and me to follow the trail of the stolen animals and track down and capture or kill the rest of the raiding party.

So I know about the terrible attack upon my people only from what I saw myself at the bloody scene when it was all over and from what others have told me. The few relatives who survived the massacre told me how my family died. Years later, Captain John Bourke, General Crook's long-time aide who was also an author, told me what he remembered about the attack. He also said that he felt sad about all the unfair things that the white men did to my people. I now tell the story of what happened on that dreadful day—nearly sixty years ago—mostly from what I remember hearing from others.

The night before the attack, my father and other warriors from Nanni-Chaddi's band returned home from a raid upon Pima settlements in the Gila Valley with six horses and nine mules. Because the animals were unable to climb the rocky trail up the canyon wall, it was necessary to leave all but one in the pasture. As the warriors began to butcher an animal that they might carry the meat on their backs to their hungry families, Uncle Meesakauwa joined them.

By the time the animal was slaughtered, my uncle had told the sad story about my capture and warned that many troops were in the area. The men hurried to Nanni-Chaddi's cave where they knew they would be safe.

Nantje led the small party of sharp shooters up a narrow, winding trail until they were within a few feet of the summit. They then turned and headed down the slippery cliff that formed the canyon wall. When they reached a shelf in the steep cliff, Nantje pointed toward the left to the shallow cave in the canyon wall.

Only a few yards away in an open space before the cave, several warriors were dancing and singing—celebrating their successful raid and asking for my safe return. The troopers quickly took positions behind the rocks. Ross ordered each man to quietly cock his weapon, pick a target, aim, and fire.

My people were so busy praising and praying to Sakarakaamche and their singing was so loud that they did not hear the low whisper, "Ready! Aim! Fire!" But they heard the terrible roar of the bullets poured upon them by Ross and his sharpshooters. Six warriors met almost instant death, and the others were so surprised and terrified that they ran for the safety of the cave. My dear old grandfather was among the first to die on that terrible day.

Major Brown also heard the loud noise that echoed throughout the usually quiet canyon. Brown sent Captain Bourke and forty more men to join the sharpshooters.

The two detachments, totaling fifty-five men, united and secured their positions within thirty yards of the cave. Bourke ordered his men to remain hidden behind the rocks and to take part in the fight only if the hostiles tried to escape.

Uncle Meesakauwa, believing that I had led the soldiers to the fortress, felt responsible for the attack and decided to run for help. He said to his frightened wife, "We are trapped. Unless help comes, we will all die. I must get word to Delche."

"Soldiers do not listen to so small a boy," she said. "If you leave the cave, the soldiers will kill you."

My uncle slipped quietly from the cave, crept down along the right side of the soldiers, and was not seen until he climbed upon a rock where he made a perfect target. Within seconds Uncle Meesakauwa fell from the rock. My people's only hope had a bullet through his heart.

Many times Major Brown asked my people to surrender and promised to treat them kindly. The Indians always replied with shrieks of hatred and defiance. The white men had told so many lies and had broken so many promises that Nanni-Chaddi, my father and the others did not believe the words of Major Brown's interpreter. They did not know that my uncle was dead and believed that they were safe in their cave until Delche came to their rescue.

Suddenly, after a long lull in the fighting, the soldiers fired hundreds of bullets toward the cave's ceiling that ricocheted in all directions killing Chief Nanni-Chaddi and many warriors. The angry survivors rapidly returned the fire with more arrows and a few bullets.

Major Brown and Captain Bourke heard the little children's shrieks and the little babies' weak cries; they heard the wailing of their mothers. Brown again ordered a cease-fire and asked the warriors to allow the women and children to leave the cave.

After several moments of silence, the Indians began their war chant. My father and other warriors charged from the cave. They did not know that forty soldiers waited behind the first firing line. All were shot down.

After a long, tiring, march over the mountain, Major Burns, the men of Company G and I returned to rejoin Major Brown's forces. Everybody but me was mad that we had found no sign of another raiding party. I kept hoping that Delche and his men had come to rescue my family.

We came to the spot overlooking the Salt River Canyon and directly above Nanni-Chaddi's cave—the place where I had last seen my grandfather and my little brother and baby sister. When we heard the terrible commotion below us, Burns and several others leaned over the wall to see what the frightful racket was about.

Burns made a quick decision and prepared for action. He pulled me back from the canyon wall. Two sharp shooters were harnessed in place by their comrades' suspenders. They then leaned far over the wall and fired their revolvers at the few Indians who still defended the cave. Brown's men continued to fire their volleys at the sides and ceiling of the cave.

All the warriors were now dead or dying, and only our old medicine man continued to defend his people. Wearing feathers on his head and a shirt decorated with all the sacred objects of my people, he defied death and kept firing at everything that moved on the enemy's side of the rampart. One woman and a young boy remained at his side reloading rifles and handing them back.

Captain Burns ordered his men to roll large boulders over the precipice down on the helpless Indians. The stone wall collapsed and shattered from the crashing rocks, and the old medicine man and his two helpers were crushed to death instantly by a single crashing boulder. There was soon silence below.

At twelve o'clock noon, Major Brown signaled a cease-fire, and his soldiers entered the fortress from each side of the rampart. The men of G Troop were lowered two at a time by ropes to the place of death.

I was lowered to the cave. Everywhere I saw only dead men, women and children—all bloody and horrible to look at. Someone counted seventy-six bodies, including many little children and tiny babies. All the warriors were dead or dying. Thirty-five living people left the cave, many with fatal injuries. Several women and their children had hidden behind and under large slabs of stone. Some women had piled up the dead to protect themselves and their children.

Nantje identified the dead and told me that both my father and uncle had fought bravely. He said that if my uncle had made it to another Yavapai village, the outcome of the attack might have been different—little comfort to a poor orphaned child. Nantje showed me where my dear old grandfather lay dead. He had been among the first to die. My little brother and sister, my aunt and three of her children were dead, but—unknown to me at the time—my two oldest cousins had survived. Just before daylight, the sisters and four other young girls went out to check the mescal roasting in nearby ovens.

I behaved like the normal child I was. Thinking of my old grandfather and my little brother and baby sister, I sat down and cried. "They never hurt anybody," I howled. "No more hope, no more family. What shall I do—give myself up to be killed by the Pimas? Oh would someone tell me what to do."

Looking around and hoping for an answer, I noticed the Pima scouts gathered around their dead friend—the only fatality on the army's side. They were crying even harder than I was. So I thought it best to stop crying and get away while they were mourning lest they come and beat me to death with their clubs.

I am rather ashamed to tell what happened to the inhabitants of the cave. It still brings tears to my eyes to mention it, because in this place my father and his two children, my aunt and uncle and five children, and my poor grandfather were slaughtered with many other relatives. I am now the only one of my family still alive.

12
Scouting with the Fifth Cavalry
January — February 1873

Without bothering to bury the dead, the soldiers and their captives left the bloody scene in the Salt River Canyon. Many captives were so badly injured they could not walk, and the soldiers carried them. One woman, too seriously wounded to be moved, was given food and water and left behind. When the soldiers were out of sight, two Pimas went back and finished her off with their clubs. No grown men were taken alive at all. If the Pimas had not rushed into the caves and crushed the heads of those nearly dead, there might have been more captives.

Only eighteen of the thirty-five captives survived the trek out of the canyon. Perhaps some would still be alive if a doctor had been along to save them. Often in those days, no doctors went with soldiers on their campaigns, and they had no medical supplies—not even bandages. Luckily, for the Fifth Cavalry only the Pima scout died.

The whole command marched toward the Mazatzal Mountains and camped by a small spring in the foothills, the place where we had left our pack trains and horses. During the night, three more captives died. When we set out early the next morning, Captain Burns ordered the Apache-Mohave scouts to go ahead with the prisoners to Fort McDowell and not to let the Pimas or Maricopas near them. He warned the Pimas that the Apache-Mohave scouts would shoot them if they bothered the captives. Two messengers rode to Camp Grant to tell General Crook of the victory over Nanni-Chaddi's tribe. Two others hurried to Fort McDowell to tell the post commander that wounded prisoners would be coming in soon.

We followed Sycamore Creek to the Verde River, which we crossed and followed to Fort McDowell. Toward evening we arrived at the post and found the captives safe and well guarded near the horse corral.

At times I was so lonely for my family that I wished I had died with them, but most of the time I was grateful for the kind treatment from my captors. I even began to believe I had been rescued.

Soon after my arrival at Fort McDowell, Lieutenant Thomas brought Gai-am-am-a (Going By), a boy about my age who had survived the massacre, to the post. He was a relative I had not known well before the massacre. He and his family had arrived at Nanni-Chaddi's cave a week before the massacre—about the time I had left with my uncle. They had come there to be safe from the enemy.

Gaiamama had two flesh wounds that were not serious. His father had died; but his mother, a married sister and two more children were taken alive. Each night, Gaiamama slept between two soldiers detailed to look after him. One was the cook, and the other one—I think now—used to care for the officers' horses. In those days, I did not know much about what was happening. I always slept in a tent nearby with Captain Burns. I enjoyed Gaiamama's company for a while. Each day, we went to the camp where the captives were held and guarded. Gaiamama stayed with his mother and sister nearly all day long. I had no one to visit so I never stayed long, and I returned to the post by myself or with soldiers.

The captives were held at Fort McDowell for two weeks. I became used to having Gaiamama—someone my age who spoke my language—around every night, and I thought he would always stay and be company for me. Gaiamama told me once that Lieutenant Thomas liked him and wanted to make him his boy. But one morning, I missed Gaiamama and went to the camp where his mother and sister stayed. To my great surprise, there were no Indians in the camp. I felt so very lonely. I had talked to these people nearly every day and had become a little more satisfied with my situation. "Where have they gone to?" I asked myself. "What has become of them? Would the soldiers be so heartless as to give these poor innocent women and children up to the Pimas—to be butchered up like the rest of my people in that cave? Were they sold as slaves?" I was not able then to speak English or Mexican, so I could not find out what became of Gaiamama and my other relatives.

The next week after many more captives were brought to Fort McDowell, Company G was ordered to take the prisoners to the San Carlos Indian Reservation. The first night as we were setting up camp, scouts brought in more captives. To my surprise I saw a young Indian woman with a small baby strapped to her back whom I had seen before. She recognized me and said she was my cousin. Her people were from the upper part of the Superstition Mountains. One month earlier, they were on their way to the cave where all my people had died. The next day, they would have been in that cave; but they were on the wrong side of the Salt River, which was too high at the time to cross. They moved down the river bank to gather greens and seeds, as they had no other food, and waited for the water to lower.

My cousin told me that one man in her party scouted ahead of the others and learned that enemies had attacked the cave. The next day, a few young men managed to cross the river to see what had become of their relatives. When they returned, they told about the horrible sight—a large cave full of murdered men, women and children. They gave up the notion of going across the river and moved down to the south side watching out for soldiers and Pimas. The older men thought the soldiers had gone home and would not return to this country again after they had killed so many.

While the women were alone on the river bank gathering greens, scouts of our own people came upon them. The women without children ran off and got away, but the scouts had easily overtaken my cousin with a baby strapped to her back.

After she told me her story, I began to cry. "I am the only one left in my family," I sobbed. "Almost everyone in the band of Nanni-Chaddi is dead. Just a few were captured. They have gone away, and I know not where. I have no more family. Men from our own people led the white soldiers to our cave. I would be lying there dead if soldiers had not captured me first." I still did not know that two cousins—the oldest daughters of my Uncle Meesakauwa—still lived.

Two days later, a scout came to me and said that the woman with a child on her back had left the camp. He asked if she had told me where she was going. I told him that she had not. She was my cousin, and I thought she would stay to comfort me as she was as lonely as I was. Now she was gone, and no one knew where to hunt her. I was the only one left from a large tribe of Indians.

Captain Burns took the many bands of captives to San Carlos where they were to settle and draw rations. While I camped close to the river with the soldiers, some of my people, the Apache-Mohaves, who are really Yavapais, came to see me. They asked me to get some ammunition for them. I wondered why they expected that the soldiers would give any ammunition to a small boy like me. The soldiers would not trust me with any because they knew I could not use it, and I would only want to give it away to other Indians. So I told them not to ask me for any more cartridges.

More Yavapais came around the camp—close to Captain Burns' tent where I always slept—crying and insisting that I leave the soldiers' camp. They promised that if I came to their camp, the whole band would move off toward the Superstitions and Four Peaks—to our old camping grounds. One visitor was my cousin, Mat-taw-she (Wind) who had lived with us when my mother was alive. After my mother was killed, he went off to get married and lived with Indians who roamed around the Pinal Mountains. Mattawshe begged me to leave the soldiers and come to his place. He said that the next day he would take me away up to the top of a mountain to hide.

I said, "You ought to know that I have no father, nor mother, nor uncle, nor aunt, and that my little brother and my baby sister whom I loved so much were all killed. I have no living relatives that I can live with after reaching the country where my people used to live."

A few weeks later, Captain Burns' command moved to higher ground and camped near a village of Arivaipa and Pinal Apaches—these were real Apaches—and Apache-Mohaves. Here we stayed for about three weeks. Every day, Indians came and begged me to leave the soldiers. Some said that the soldiers were going to sell me off to some Pimas; others said that the soldiers were going to kill me. I decided that it was time to leave and join my people again.

I always slept with Captain Burns. He made me lie next to the wall of the tent, so he would be in front of me. During the day while no one was watching, I loosened the tent sticks right behind where I always lay. About midnight when the whole camp was quiet and the captain was sound asleep, I put a blanket out under one corner of the tent, quietly crawled under the cover, and stepped off into the darkness toward the Apache-Mohave camp.

Each time I came to a hut, I listened carefully to detect the language they spoke and what people they were. I passed several camps before I came to one where I clearly understood every word spoken. But when I listened carefully to their voices, I knew they were not the party I was hunting. I was looking for my cousin Mattawshe, the one who begged me to leave the camp and live with his people.

At last I came to Mattawshe's hut. It was not much of a hut because they had just recently arrived and expected to leave soon. My cousin took me to the chief who was also a cousin. But Chief Ya-ca-watch-ha feared the real Apaches who were more numerous than the Apache-Mohaves. He said, "If the Apaches give me away for hiding captives from the soldiers, I will likely be put to death for the act. You must go back to the soldiers' camp and stay with them as long as you can. It is not good to come back to the Indians again, for there are no close relatives left for you to live with." My cousin cried while Yacawatchha was talking, but he agreed with his chief. I cried and went away.

I made up my mind to heed no more foolish advice. When I reached Captain Burns' tent, I listened carefully, heard him snoring loudly, crept in the same way I came out, and lay there quietly. The next morning I was scared that I might be whipped for being absent nearly all night. Luckily, no one ever has known a thing about my running away that night.

In February, Company G left San Carlos for Fort Whipple where we remained for several days. While at San Carlos, someone had made me a little soldier's suit—so I was dressed as tidily as any soldier. I had also learned the soldiers' ways. When I met officers, I always saluted them, and they did the same.

When all the soldiers were paid but me, the company bugler led me to a room where several officers sat. I stood up straight with head up and hands on each side of my body. When the officers began to laugh, I could not understand why and felt like crying; but I just stood there, shaking a little, until one man handed me some money. I did not know how much it was, because in those days I did not know the value of money. I learned later that I was paid one dollar and fifty-four cents.

After being paid, Captain Burns and Lieutenant Thomas and the command marched up the big pine mountain west of Prescott and went down to Skull Valley where we camped. That evening Captain Burns handed me a piece of white paper, and a green paper too. Then he pointed to a house a little distance from the camp. So I ran off to the house. A man met me there, and I handed him both papers—one, I now suppose, was money. He kept the papers, gave me some eggs, and I ran quickly back to camp.

I noticed both officers were laughing, but by then I was used to their laughs and ignored them. Then suddenly, Burns began to talk loudly and went off to get a stick. I continued to ignore him until, all at once, he came toward me with the stick in his hand and swearing. When he struck me on my back end, I began to dance around and cry. While I was being punished—for what, I did not know—the man who took the papers and gave me the eggs came running into our camp. He went right up to Burns, handed him something, and soon they both were talking and laughing. I feared that the captain would strike me again with that large stick in his hand until at last I saw him throw it away. After that I was not so scared to get a whipping.

Captain Burns must have given me either a five or a ten dollar bill. He expected me to get the change back. But he ought to have known better than that. I was not civilized enough to know different kinds of money, and I could not then have known how much eggs were worth.

13
Camp Date Creek
February — April 1873

Captain Burns and I arrived at Camp Date Creek in February 1873. This was not a pretty place like the country I came from, but here for the first time since my capture, I was sometimes happy.

The post was built upon a rocky slope half surrounded by high rocky hills and about seven hundred yards from a muddy, slow-moving creek. The post and the creek got their names from the thick growth of yucca on the far side of the creek. The fruit grows in clusters like dates, looks and tastes like bananas, and is very good to eat when roasted. In the springtime, white flowers grow on the strong high stalks and smell so sweet at night.

In 1864, about a year before I was born, soldiers set up camp near Date Creek to protect the white farmers in Skull Valley and travelers along the road between Prescott and Ehrenberg from dangerous Indians. In July 1870, two Tolkopaya from O-cho-co-ma's band came to the post asking for peace and protection from the white settlers who had stolen their lands and were now shooting them on sight. The Tolkopaya were called Apache-Yumas by the white men. They were Yavapais from western Arizona whose speech was much like that of my people, the Kwoyokopaya. The post commander Captain O'Bierne agreed, and he promised good treatment if they were peaceful. As peaceful Indians, he said, they were free to roam over the mountains near the post to hunt game and gather wild fruits, but they must stay away from the roads leading to Prescott, Wickenburg and Ehrenberg. O'Bierne gave them some rations, and the soldiers gave them their cast-off clothing. In October 1871, General George Crook made Date Creek a temporary reservation and ordered the quartermaster to give rations to the peaceful and needy Indians. All Indians off the reservation were at war.

After General Crook's army destroyed their food supply and killed or captured so many Yavapais, Chiefs Je-maspie, Ochocama, Che-wha-ja-ka-ma—who later was called Captain Snooks—and over 2,000 Tolkopaya came to the reservation asking for peace and rations. Doctor William Corbusier arrived at Date Creek in early January 1873. The doctor soon became very interested in the Indians' health and well-being. He made many friends among them and tended to their needs at Date Creek and later at Fort Verde.

About noon on a very warm February day, Captain James Burns and I arrived at the Corbusier's jacal, a brush shelter that separated their two-room adobe house from the kitchen and dining room. In warm weather, the jacal kept some heat from the house, and two large porous earthen jars, called ollas, that kept water cool hung there. The doctor's jacal was the headquarters for hearing the news of the day, and new arrivals first stopped there. Fortunately, the ollas were full when we arrived, and we each enjoyed a drink of cool refreshing water.

The Corbusiers were the first white family I ever knew. Captain Burns and Doctor Corbusier were always busy and did not have much time for me, so I spent many daytime hours with Mrs. Fanny Corbusier. She had two small children. Hal was just a few weeks old, and I did not pay much attention to him. But Claude was about two years old, and I took to him at once. I could even understand his baby English, and I think he understood me. I helped Mrs. Corbusier by watching him like I once had my own little brother.

Mrs. Corbusier was very kind to me. She treated me like an older son. For some reason she did not like to call me Mike, and she always called me Hoomothya. Mrs. Corbusier took time to teach me English. I was rather slow at first, but she was very patient. She never laughed at me when I did something stupid because I was still not quite civilized and did not understand the customs of white people. I soon learned many words in English and the proper ways of the white man. I quickly became very good at using a knife and fork.

I wondered at how different the white woman's life was from the life of an Indian woman. White men did women's work. They carried wood from the post wood pile and water from the nearby stream. After I got to know the family, carrying wood and water became my job. Once, I thought how the Indian boys from my village would laugh if they saw me doing women's work; then I remembered that these boys were dead. A big yellow-haired man named Sorenson, who came from a place called Sweden, did the cooking. I sometimes longed for my mother's mescal and bread made from mesquite seeds and piñon nuts and wondered if the food would taste better if Mrs. Corbusier did the cooking

Mrs. Corbusier told me about the good foods she had enjoyed back in New York State, especially the fresh vegetables from the family garden and the fruits from the orchard. A few years later, I would get to see these wonderful Eastern gardens and orchards for myself. The post garden was not successful so we had few fresh vegetables, mostly canned or dried foods to eat.

One day, I accompanied the doctor on a trip to the Hassayampa River. I pointed out the watercress growing in a shallow pool. "Good," I said nibbling on a tender leaf. The doctor agreed, and we returned home with several plants. Some soldiers planted them in the creek near the quarters, and very soon everyone on the post enjoyed watercress.

Mrs. Corbusier begged for a cow so that Claude and I could enjoy fresh milk instead of the sweet stuff in a can that she mixed with water. I was unable to explain that I, like other little Indian boys, had never drank milk since I was weaned from my mother's breast. The doctor borrowed a cow from Charles Genung's ranch, and he hired a soldier to milk her. The cow, which was wild and had never been milked, did not cooperate. At the first pull, she upset the milker and the pail, tore down the fence, and headed back toward the range and freedom. It was years later when I was milking cows in New York State that I enjoyed the taste of fresh milk, and I remembered the happy days with Mrs. Fanny Corbusier.

When Captain Burns stayed at Date Creek, I slept with him in his tent and spent the days with Mrs. Corbusier. When Burns went into the field after renegade Indians, I stayed with Mrs. Thomas, wife of Lieutenant Earl Thomas —the officer who named me Mike and persuaded Captain Burns to adopt me. My job was to care for the chickens. I did the job of a soldier who was now on a scout with Captain Burns, and I felt very grown up and important. I got plenty of exercise carrying water from the water wagon to the chickens. A well had been dug for drinking water, but most water used by the post was hauled in barrels by wagon from a creek about a mile away. One soldier acted as guard over the soldier-prisoners who did the work. When a wagon came to the house, I filled a bucket and ran over the hill to fill the little cans in the bushes where the chickens were.

I also enjoyed my new freedom, and often I ran over the next hill to visit the Tolkopaya in their village near the creek. I could talk to them because they spoke the same language as my people, the Kwoyokopaya. Many little boys and girls lived in the village, and nearly every day I played with them. One old man made me a small bow and some arrows so I could shoot at targets with the other children. I had so much fun with the Indian children that I often stayed at the camp nearly all day long. Sometimes I stayed there past the time when Mrs. Thomas wanted me. When she could not find me, she sent soldiers to hunt me down. They always found me at the Indian camp and rushed me back to the post.

The Tolkopaya often asked me about where I came from and how I happened to be with the soldiers. I told them that my people used to live near Four Peaks. I did not like to tell them that my people were all killed in a cave, nor did I even like to mention that terrible affair because it always made me unhappy and want to cry.

One day when Captain Burns and Lieutenant Thomas and their command were out on the desert for nearly a month, I was gathering the chickens that were scattered over the hills. Suddenly, I noticed a long column of men coming over the distant hills about a mile and a half away. In four rows they came, some on horses and some on foot. For a long time, I stood watching to make sure what I saw was real. In my excitement, I forgot the chickens and ran over the hill to the Thomas' quarters. I tried to tell the news to Mrs. Thomas, but I forgot all the English words. I could only make some motions and point over the hills shouting, "Indians! Indians!"

Poor Mrs. Thomas was scared. She thought that wild Indians were coming to attack the garrison, and few soldiers were there to protect it. She rushed to the guard house. The soldiers quickly grabbed their guns and headed toward the hills.

Captain Burns and Lieutenant Thomas were coming in with more than five hundred of my people, the Kwoyo-kopaya. The soldiers called them Apache-Mohaves. They camped near the river close to the Tolkopaya. Now there were many more children and many new playmates. I was nearly eight years old, and I was happy most of the time.

Later, other Indians came in from the western part of Arizona. Their leader was Pa-ko-tay (Big Man) or Nya-kwa-la-hwa-la (Long Black Fellow) afterwards called José Coffee by the white men.

14
Pakotay Visits Washington
June — September 1872

I must tell the story of Pakotay's trip to Washington that began about a year before I came to Camp Date Camp. He told me about it nearly twenty years later when we both lived at San Carlos. I tell it now because his story helps make sense of what happened later.

General Oliver Howard was the one-armed general who wanted to help the Indians and bring peace between his people and mine. In the spring of 1872, he came to Arizona to choose Indians from many tribes to visit President Ulysses Grant in Washington. General Howard; his aide-de-camp, Captain Wilkinson; Superintendent of Indian Affairs, Mr. Bendell; Dr. Cook, the Pima missionary and teacher; Joe Gacka, the Yavapais' interpreter; and about a dozen soldiers arrived at Camp Date Creek in early June.

Four Indians arrived with Howard's party. Two were from Camp Grant. Santo, a former Arivaipa Apache chief, was the father of Chief Eskiminzin's three wives. Conception Equierre was a Mexican half-breed who spoke Spanish, Apache and English. Two were Pimas. Antoneto was the son of Chief Antonio Azul. Louis could translate from English into Spanish and from Spanish into Pima. These Indians wanted peace with all the other Indians and with the white men too.

There was much talking, but no Apache-Yuma chief would agree to go with the white man. Chief Ochocoma had many bad experiences as a result of the white men's broken promises. "I fear," he said, "if I go to see the big white chief, I will never come back."

Chief Jemaspie said, "If the big white chief wants to talk to me, let him come to my village."

Finally, two young men, Pakotay and his nephew, Tako-da-wa (Hanging on a Limb), agreed to represent the Apache-Yumas. Pakotay and Takodawa were not chiefs yet, but they were good choices to represent their people. Sometime in June 1872, they climbed aboard a large army ambulance and began their long journey across the United States.

Howard's party camped the first night in Skull Valley, and the next day they reached Fort Whipple where the Indians received clothing for the long journey. As they camped near Fort Verde, Joe Gacka came from the post with three Yavapai prisoners and their soldier guards. The prisoners told Pakotay that three months earlier they had come from the hills to make peace. They asked that when their people came in, they would not be harmed. Without any good reason, the three men were put in the guardhouse where they had stayed for three months.

When Pakotay heard this he was very upset. He remembered Chief Ochocoma's words, "I will never come back." So he went to Major Julius Mason, the Camp Verde commander, and gave him the papers from the President that called the Indians throughout the land to a peace conference in Washington. That afternoon, the three Yavapais were released and told to go out and bring in their people.

At Camp Apache, three White Mountain Apaches named Es-kel-te-ce-la, One-eyed Meguil and Pedro joined

the Yavapais, the Pimas and the Arivaipas. After seven
days, General Howard's party reached the Rio Grande opposite Albuquerque. The river was high, and the party
waited three days until a crew of Mexicans came with flat-
boats. Nine fearful Indians, who never before had traveled
by water, needed much encouragement by their white companions to board a flatboat. The three teams and the ambu-
lances and all the passengers crossed in safety, but in the
middle of the stream a great wave overturned the boat with
the three big supply wagons. The men and animals swam to
the shore; but the wagons, all the supplies and all the food
and clothing went down the river, never to be seen again.

For two days, they traveled against the angry current as
far as Santa Fe where General Howard went around the
town and bought more supplies. The Indians changed into
their new white man's clothing and boarded a stage just like
white men.

North of Pueblo, Colorado, the Indians had another big
surprise. They stared in wonder at all the cars and the
strange road of rails. Excitedly, they climbed into the coach
and took their seats as General Howard directed. But as the
whistle began to blow and the coach began to move slowly
and noisily down the tracks, they fell to the floor and hid in
terror between the seats until the general persuaded them
that they were in no danger.

After their fear of the train disappeared, Pakotay and
the others began to count the mountains so they might find
their way back home. When the mountains disappeared and
they saw only flat land, they decided they had no choice but
to place their trust in General Howard. Although they saw
many new and interesting sights on their long journey, by
the time Pakotay and the others finally reached Washington,
they had grown tired of riding on the crowded, sooty train
and sleeping on the hard, cold floor.

As it was summer vacation in the nation's capital, the Indians stayed in the dormitories of Howard University, the university that General Howard had started for black students. They had their meals at Howard's house nearby. Pakotay was eager to visit the President—the purpose of the long journey—that it all might be soon over and he could return home. It was two weeks before the general could get an appointment for the delegates to see the President. Pakotay could not remember how they got through the terrible waiting time.

One morning, General Howard came to their dormitory room and told them to bathe and dress quickly as they were going to see the President at last. Pakotay dressed as hastily as he could, but he had a hard time getting into the strange, new clothing. Finally, he put on the fancy feathered headdress that the government had given him.

Pakotay did not know what to think when he saw so many soldiers in front of a large white building. They went up some steps and saw more soldiers—then up some more steps and still more soldiers. "Are all those soldiers with guns there just to keep ten Indians with only feathers and no guns from causing trouble?" he asked Takodawa.

Finally, they came to the room where President Grant sat at his desk. The President rose, shook hands with the Indians, and asked them to be seated. He was a short fat man with a short beard. President Grant did not look like the big white chief of Pakotay's imagination.

President Grant said, "I have sent for you that you may know that there must be peace in all America. I have made peace with the people of the South, and now I want peace with all Indians." Pakotay asked himself, "Who are the people of the South?"

The President continued, "As long as you remain on your reservations, I will give you rations and clothing. I want to send your children to school and educate them like white children. But all who do not listen and refuse to stay on the reservation and become farmers will be punished."

President Grant chose these Arizona Indians to be chiefs of their people, and he gave each Indian a paper with a lot of strange writing and a medal with the President's picture on it. The President then said that the emissaries should show the paper and the medal to any of their people who did not believe their stories. The President does not know the customs of our people, Pakotay thought. No white man, not even the big white chief himself, can choose our chiefs. My paper is worthless because no one in my tribe can read it. Chief Jemaspie was right. The President should come to the Yavapai villages. Then he would know our customs and our needs.

Finally, President Grant gave each delegate a paper worth fifty dollars, but Pakotay and the others did not know what to do with it. Twenty years later, Pakotay said to me, "We took the papers and the medal, but you can see that all I have left after all these years is the medal. I wear poor clothes and have no chance to hunt deer and only sad memories of the days when we roamed the mountains."

The Indians visited many places, always wearing their feathered headdresses flowing down their backs. The Easterners stared at them. They visited many large cities and saw the crowds of people in the streets and the large and splendid buildings. He wondered, how so many people could like living so close together where there was always noise and commotion. After he saw the hundreds of ships in the harbors and walked through the place where many large guns were stored, Pakotay understood the great power of the United States. He said to Takodawa, "We must never fight the white men again."

When they attended a Peace Society meeting, Mr. Vincent Colyer listened carefully to all that the Indians had to say. "Mr. Colyer is a true friend," Pakotay said to the others. "He has visited our people." But Mr. Colyer was not as powerful as the President.

The trip to New York, Philadelphia, and back to Washington became very tiresome and boring, and Pakotay became increasingly anxious to return to his people. He told me that he was tired of looking at so many things and always going someplace. "No sleep—no rest—too much to see—just go—all the time go," he said. "I wanted to go home and look at the blue sky and the clouds and the stars at night."

After more than three months visiting Eastern cities, Pakotay was finally on his way home. In San Francisco, Pakotay threw away his Indian headdress. Takodawa wanted to keep his, but Pakotay said, "We will soon be back in Indian country and no longer chiefs. Our people will laugh at us if they see us with all those feathers."

After a short stay in San Francisco, Doctor McNulty, Doctor Cook, the three Pimas, the two Yavapais and their military escort traveled by steamer through the Gulf of California and up the Colorado River. At Fort Yuma they boarded a stage for home.

15
Pakotay's Return
September 1872

Pakotay's home coming was more disappointing than his journey. Few Indians were camped by the river near Camp Date Creek, and they acted angry and suspicious. They called Takodawa, later to be known as Washington Charlie, a liar, and he soon stopped telling about all the wonders he had seen. Pakotay wore his medal and showed his letter from the President, which no one including himself could read.

When they learned of the great wrong done to their people, Pakotay and Takodawa understood their strange behavior. They found out about the great tragedy the same day they returned from their long journey to visit President Grant who had said there would always be peace between the United States and the Indians.

It all started in November 1871 when General Crook got word that Indians had attacked the Wickenburg to Ehrenberg stage and had killed the driver and five of the seven passengers. Mohave chiefs I-ra-ta-ba, Na-ta-daw-va, and A-wah-so-sit-saw were envious of the Apache-Yumas camped at Date Creek and blamed the killing on them.

Captain James Burns, the post commander, believed the Apache-Yumas were innocent. He had told the Indians they must not leave camp without a written pass stating the purpose for leaving. No one had come for such permission. They had been counted every week for months, and no absentees had been reported. Mr. Charles Genung also believed them to be innocent.

Earlier that year, Genung had hired thirty Date Creek Indians to build a road from his a ranch in Peeple's Valley to link with the road between Ehrenberg and Phoenix. Genung knew that on the day of the massacre, his Indians were at work on the road and that they did not commit the crime.

But General Crook believed that some Date Creek Indians were guilty. Nearly one year after the murder on the Wickenburg stage and at the time when Pakotay was on his way home, General Crook ordered all the Date Creek warriors to gather on the parade ground and enlist as scouts in the United State Army. On the appointed day, only Chief Ochocoma and fifty-two young men of his band appeared. Because several Indians had died during a malaria and whooping cough epidemic, Agent Josephus Williams had permitted many survivors to leave for the healthier mountains.

General Crook, Captain Bourke, Lieutenant Ross and Commissioner of Indian Affairs Herman Bendell sat in front of the headquarters building. Chiefs Irataba, Natadawva, Awahsositsaw and several Mohave warriors sat just in front of the general's party. The Yavapais sat on benches or stood facing the white men and the Mohaves. Twenty of the general's soldiers stood among the Indians. Captain Burns and G Troop stood to the left of the crowd.

Charlie Spencer, Irataba's interpreter, said to the Yavapais, "General Crook has asked you to come here today to make a lasting peace." Then, two of Irataba's men got up and began to pass tobacco to the Yavapais. Suddenly, the Mohaves stopped and stood aside, and the soldiers who stood among the Indians, drew their revolvers and grabbed the Indians who had received the tobacco.

Genung protested loudly that the Indians had been set up. As the frightened Yavapais struggled desperately to escape, Crook's soldiers fired at them with revolvers. Captain Burns ordered the soldiers to stop shooting but was unsuccessful. The other officers took no action, but stood silently and watched the fracas.

One Indian pulled out a knife and stabbed a soldier. Another grabbed the wounded soldier's gun and aimed it at General Crook. Lieutenant Ross, responding quickly to the danger, pushed Crook out of the way just as the gun went off. The bullet hit another Indian. As the Date Creek Indians fled from the parade ground, the soldiers from Fort Whipple fired at them until they were out of sight.

Eight Yavapais lay dead, and many others were wounded. Three soldiers grabbed Chief Ochocoma and dragged him to the guard house. Again the chief had been deceived by white men. The surviving Indians fled with their families to the mountains. Ochocoma soon managed to escape and joined them.

After Pakotay heard about the murder of his people, he went to Captain James Burns and showed him the paper from President Grant and the medal with the President's face on it. Captain Burns studied the paper carefully. He was sorry for the things that had been done to Pakotay's people. Burns wanted him to understand that he and his command were not to blame for this tragedy. Burns did not believe that any Date Creek Indians had committed the crime, and he had reported this belief to his superiors. Unfortunately, General Crook believed the lies told by the Mohave villains, and he let those innocent men die right in front of their own people.

Pakotay and Takodawa joined their people in the mountains. By October 1872, few Indians remained camped

outside Date Creek Camp. Lieutenant Volkmer, who was
the post commander at the time, sent word through their
good friend Charles Genung that he wanted them back.
Volkmer had orders to feed and protect any returning fugi-
tives. General George Crook was about to go on the warpath in earnest, and off-reservation Indians would be considered the enemy.

Most Apache-Yumas did return—hungry and cold and
tired of being hunted down like animals. General Crook
held another conference and gained the trust of many Date
Creek Indians. Several young men agreed to enlist as
scouts, and the general promised to care for the women,
children and old men left behind on the reservation.

The tribes of Chief Ochocoma, Jemaspie and Pakotay,
who had so often experienced the white men's unfaithful-
ness, hid out in the remote canyons and mountains for several months until Captain Burns and Doctor Corbusier persuaded them, in the spring of 1873, that it was safe to return. Pakotay's band was the last to return.

About May 1, 1873 Chiefs Jemaspie and Ochocoma
and their bands were sent to the Colorado River. The remaining Date Creek Indians—all the Apache-Mohaves and
most Apache-Yumas—went to Camp Verde to live with
many other Yavapai bands.

That was a very sad morning for me when I saw about
eight hundred Yavapais lined up in columns on the post parade ground. They marched out of the camp, escorted by
Doctor Williams, Captain George F. Price and Company E,
Fifth Cavalry, and headed northeast toward the Verde
River. I cried when I saw the Indians leave. I feared I would
never see them again. I never again played with children of
my own people, with children who spoke my own language.
Years later at San Carlos, when we had grown up, I became
reacquainted with many of them. By that time Pakotay was

an important Apache-Yuma chief and a scout for the United States Army called José Coffee.

Captain Burns and Doctor Corbusier had to stay behind to close up Camp Date Creek. Just before I left with Captain Burns for Fort Whipple, Chief Delche visited the post. I often wondered what had happened to my people's greatest chief, and I thought that by this time he was probably dead. Although I only got a glimpse of him, I recognized Delche at once.

Delche and his band came to Date Creek asking for food and medicine. Doctor Corbusier did not like Delche very much. Years later he told me that Delche was the only Indian he could not trust. He said he was a big trouble maker. Doctor Corbusier had heard about him from other white men so he did not really understand the Indian side of the story. At the time of Crook's big campaign, Delche was General Crook's most wanted Indian. I think that Delche did some very bad things, but he was blamed for many things that he did not do. General Crook and Doctor Corbusier did not know about all the bad things that the white men did to Delche and his people and why Delche could not trust them.

I was too afraid of Delche to speak to him. I was still a small child, and he was the largest Indian I had ever seen. One member of his band, a boy about my age, told me the story. When Chalipun and most of the Apache-Mohaves surrendered to General Crook and moved to the Verde Agency, Delche and his band continued to hide out. They did not want to live close to so many people—that was not the Indian way. Major George Randall's Apache-Mohave scouts looked everywhere in the Mazatzal and the Sierra Ancha Mountains and in the canyons in between, but they were always just behind the outlaws. Delche was never in his usual hiding places, and he never stayed long in a temporary camp. Finally, after two months of being hunted down and while his band camped in a hidden canyon on the Mogollon Rim, Randall's scouts found them. Just before dawn, the troops surrounded the camp and began firing into it. Delche surrendered; he could not escape. He had only twenty warriors left because many had joined the white soldiers in hunting him down. Randall escorted Delche and his people to Fort Apache.

Delche's band did not like living at Fort Apache. This was not their country. The Apaches spoke a different language, and they often mistreated the small Yavapai band. When the Yavapais had a chance, they escaped and headed for Date Creek. Doctor Corbusier ordered food brought to Delche and his men, and he treated them for tapeworm. He then told Delche that if he did not want to be hunted down, he should head for Fort Verde. Delche's band left as suddenly as they had arrived. I would never see the chief again, but I would hear about him.

When Camp Date Creek was closed down, Doctor Corbusier went to the Verde Reservation and Mrs. Fanny Corbusier returned to her family in Elmira, New York for a vacation. She was tearful as she kissed me good-bye. I saw the Corbusiers again when we were all much older and their four sons were grown men and my children were nearly grown. I was off with Captain Burns and Troop G to Fort Whipple and another adventure.

16
Fort Whipple
May 1873 — July 1875

In late May 1873, I went with Captain Burns and Lieutenant Thomas to Fort Whipple. Ten years earlier all the troubles for my people, the Kwoyokopaya, had begun around this place. Many deer and other wild animals lived in this beautiful, hilly country with many trees and plenty of water, and Kwoyokopaya villages were located near the many streams. Very few white men came to this country, and they never stayed for long. But in 1863—sadly for my people—white prospectors found gold on the Hassayampa River south of where Fort Whipple is now. More white men came. They built houses and planted crops where the Indians had their homes and gardens. They frightened away the deer that my people depended on for meat.

Then the army came to protect the white people from the Indians who had not done anything bad yet. Next the government came, and soon Prescott—the town next to Fort Whipple—became the white man's main city. The white men drove the Kwoyokopaya away from the land they loved. My people did not have guns yet, and they could not defend themselves against the enemy who shot at them for no reason at all. Many Kwoyokopaya joined my relatives in the Tonto Basin. They were at war with the white soldiers until General Crook forced them to surrender. When I went to Fort Whipple, most of my people lived crowded together on the Verde River reservation.

After about a month at Whipple, Burns took leave. During his absence, I stayed with Second Lieutenant Hall Bishop, a young man who had just graduated from the United States Military Academy and had been in Arizona only a few weeks. Lieutenant Bishop became a good friend and the most important person in my life for many years.

After an absence of several weeks, Captain Burns returned with his wife, Annie Burns, and a daughter named Kattie. Soon after Mrs. Burns arrived at Whipple, she gave birth to a son. I did not pay much attention to the new baby, but I helped by looking after Kattie. I cared for the little girl as if she were my sister. Mrs. Burns was very good to me and treated me like one of the family.

In the fall of 1873, Captain Burns went scouting with Troop G against the Hualapais who lived in the mountain country between the San Francisco Peaks and the Grand Canyon. The Hualapais were related to the Yavapais and spoke a Yuman language much like ours. Sometimes, the Hualapais did much mischief to the whites and blamed it on the Yavapais. Captain Burns did not take me on this scout. I stayed behind with Mrs. Burns and the two little children.

At this time, I was dressed like any civilized white boy. When Captain Burns bought anything new for his little girl to wear, he also bought me clothing. Suddenly, my shoes were too small so I ran around barefoot. I did not mind if I had shoes or boots as I had been barefoot all my life until Captain Burns adopted me. When I lived with my Yavapai family, I had nothing to wear on my whole body and no shoes to protect my feet. But I now lived a different life and had to dress somewhat decently. Mrs. Burns disliked seeing me going everywhere barefoot. One morning, she gave me a ten dollar bill and told me to go into town and buy a pair of shoes or boots.

I was eager to be on the way. It was almost time for the officers' ambulance to Prescott to come by our house. Holding the bill tightly in my hand, I hurried to catch the wagon. Prescott was the largest town I had ever seen. I was very excited to be going by myself on such an important errand. Finally, the wagon driver pulled up in front of the shop. The salesman showed me many pairs of fine looking boots, new and shining and bright. I fancied one pair so much that I did not bother to try them on. I told the man to wrap them for me and handed him the money. Without waiting for the change, I hurried to get into the wagon. I was afraid that the salesman might take them back because they looked so pretty.

When the wagon drove up to the Burns' place, I strolled off to my room in the back part of the house. I did not want Mrs. Burns to see the new boots. I feared she might say they were not the right kind or did not fit me. When she came to my room and asked me what I had bought with the ten dollars, I showed her the boots. She saw that they were size seven. I wore size four. Mrs. Burns did not look happy. She told me to put the boots on my feet. I became very anxious when I thought she did not like them. I put them on my feet and walked proudly to the room where Mrs. Burns was watching her children. She was not in her usual good humor. All I wanted was to put on the fancy looking boots. I cared nothing about the size or the price.

Mrs. Burns cared little about how the boots fit my feet. She thought about that ten dollar bill she had given me to buy a pair of shoes, and I went and bought a costly pair of boots with it and did not even wait for change. The next morning, she gave me a note to take to the store in Prescott. She told me to get on the first wagon going to Prescott or I could walk to the shoe shop. I did not lose any time. I saw no wagon coming. So off I went running in my new boots. When I entered the shoe shop, the man who had sold me the boots laughed. I handed him the note, and he went and brought me two dollars and fifty cents. So the boots must have cost seven dollars and fifty cents. I returned homeward on a run again and gave the money to Mrs. Burns.

I wore the boots all the time. They soon turned up over half my foot. Mrs. Burns said, "You have a fine looking pair of boots now. I tried to make you understand they were too large for you, but you were so anxious." After that time, she never bought anything for me again, but she always treated me like one of her own children.

When Company G returned to Fort Whipple, Captain Burns was sick. His lungs were in bad shape, and he coughed constantly. He was treated first by Doctor Davis, who always went out with General Crook, and then by Doctor Matthew, the post surgeon. Lieutenant Ross of the Twenty-third Infantry, a close friend who had been with him in all the Indian wars in Arizona, was always with Captain Burns. He was sick the whole winter. All the attention given Captain Burns by several Army doctors did not help. Then they thought a change of climate might help him. They advised him to take sick leave, to go home with his wife and children to Washington D. C.

Captain Burns left Fort Whipple by ambulance for a long journey over the rough country of Arizona and New Mexico. Six soldiers and his good friend Doctor Corbusier went with him and Mrs. Burns and the two children. They would leave him at Los Alamos where he would board a train to Washington. Captain Burns instructed Second Lieutenant Bishop to take good care of me until his return in six months.

Captain Burns adopted me into his family the same as one of his children. His father and mother lived in Ireland.

Before he was sick, he often said that he was going to take me along to his parents' home. If he had not been so sick, I do believe Burns would have taken me along to Washington and then to his native land. I also believe I would never have returned to the United States nor to Arizona to see my people.

A few weeks before he left, Burns ordered a new suit of clothes for me. It was a good, neat fit on me at first; but before long, my pants were halfway up to my knees and the vest was half way up my back. Lieutenant Bishop took me to the company's tailor, Jack Jackson, and told him to measure me out for a suit of navy blue cloth—strong enough so as not to be easily torn.

Sergeant Handley came from the same place in Ireland where Captain Burns' family lived. For that reason he treated me kindly. Every pay day, Sergeant Handley collected money from the soldiers to take care of my needs and wants. Sergeant Handley gave me candy and other things I foolishly wanted. I was treated very well by all the men and officers of Company G and was kind of a pet.

One time, many strange Indians, whose language I could understand well, came to Fort Whipple. They were Hualapai scouts for General Crook, who had just returned from scouting after renegade Yavapais, and were about to be discharged. I happened to be alone on the front porch of the soldiers' quarters when about half a dozen Hualapais gathered around me. One said, "I would like to see this lad out in the hills and I would use him up this way."

Then before I could understand the danger, this unfriendly Hualapai grabbed hold of my throat and pushed me up against a post and kept pushing me harder and harder. When I finally had a chance to make a yell, Sergeant Handley rushed out, hit the Indian on the head with his fist, kicked him over the porch, and ordered the rest to move to another place. When I came to my senses—I was nearly choked to death—and wiped the tears from my eyes, I noticed those Indians running away toward their camp over by the creek, occasionally looking back toward the barracks. I was very happy that I never saw those Indians again.

Each Sunday, some half-dozen soldiers had passes to hunt rabbits. Captain Burns had left two gray hounds, named John and Nellie, with the company; and he had given me a fine little sorrel pony to ride. I went with the crowd and the two hounds over the rolling hills toward Willow Creek. We came back with twenty-five to thirty jackrabbits, a meal for all Company G.

While we were having all kinds of good times, Captain John Bourke of the Thirty-fourth Cavalry came to see me. Two of Captain Burns' soldier escorts had brought Bourke the sad news of Burns' death. He had died after crossing the Colorado River at Navajo Springs in the fall of 1874. After he was buried at Fort Wingate, New Mexico, Mrs. Annie Burns and her two children continued the journey to Washington where her family lived. I never learned the old folks' names. I was an orphan again. I cried all day and all night at the loss of my adopted father.

Captain Bourke was a warm friend of Captain Burns and my friend, too. He, at one time, had given me a whipping because I said some swearing words. I did not know what I was saying, but Captain Bourke knew that boys should not use such words. So he punished me for it, and I always remembered and have never repeated them since. So most of the time when I talk, I do not use any bad words. Everybody could do the same if they wanted. Captain John Bourke was for many years an aide-de-camp of General Crook. Wherever General Crook went Captain Bourke went too, and I would see him again many times.

Soldiers often asked if I wanted to return to my people. I could not explain how I felt so I acted as if I had not heard them. I was satisfied to stay with Lieutenant Bishop and the

other men of Company G. I would have been lost if I had
gone back to Indian life again. I knew that I had no living
relatives left. They had all died at the cave on the Salt River.
My father, my brother and sister, an aunt and uncle with five
children, and a grandfather—all were slain. I saw no reason
to go back to the Indians just because I was an Indian. I was
well cared for by the soldiers and the officers. I needed
nothing. I had a good house to stay in, a good bed with
plenty of blankets, and plenty to eat—and I had very little
work to do. For all that comfortable living, what more could
a little boy want?

Before I continue my story I must first tell about what
happened to old Chief Delche. While I was having my own
adventures at Fort Whipple—good times and sad times—
Delche kept causing trouble on the reservation, and he got
himself in much trouble. Many years after I left Fort Whipple, I learned what happened to the most important chief of
the Yavapais from two old friends—Pakotay and Doctor
Corbusier.

Several days after leaving Date Creek, Delche and his
band arrived at the Verde Agency asking permission to
camp with their people. Lieutenant Walter Schuyler, who
was in charge of the agency, had heard many stories from
other officers about Delche and did not trust him, but he
allowed him to stay.

When Delche arrived at the Verde Agency, over 2,000
Indians were camped in the low lands. Many were unhappy
with life on the reservation. They did not like living so close
together under guard, they were not used to eating the
white man's food, and they caught diseases that were new
to them. Indians got malaria from the mosquitoes that had
bitten white people. Doctor Williams treated them the best
he could without much medicine, but many Indians died.

Every time trouble broke out at the agency, Lieutenant
Schuyler blamed Delche. One day when over three hundred

Apache-Mohaves including Chiefs Chalipun and Delche disappeared into the hills, Schuyler believed that Delche was
the leader. Smoke signals were sent up ordering the fugi-
tives to return, and a courier went out with a message that
Al Sieber, the chief of scouts, was on their trail with many
soldiers and Yavapai scouts. The runaways soon returned.
Delche's explained that the Indians had left the reservation
because they were afraid of the terrible disease that had
caused so many Indians to die. When they learned that the
soldiers were after them, they decided it was healthier to
return.

A few weeks later, when more than one hundred people
had died of malaria, many reservation Indians planned another escape. When Lieutenant Schuyler found out, he
blamed Delche and arranged to arrest him. But Schuyler's
interpreter was one of Delche's men, and he reported the
plot to the chief.

Schuyler summoned all Indian men to the agency
headquarters to collect rations and be counted. When the
lieutenant told Delche that he was under arrest and soldiers
surrounded their prisoner, Delche refused to surrender.
Schuyler pointed his gun at the defiant chief. Delche
laughed, and the lieutenant pulled the trigger. The gun failed
to fire because all the bullets had been removed. Schuyler
looked around for the interpreter, but that Indian had disappeared. Schuyler knew then that his interpreter had betrayed
him. Schuyler had his spies, and Delche, who knew the
ways of the white men had his own informers.

Luckily for Schuyler, Delche was not in charge for
long. A young chief named Captain Charlie and about one
hundred young warriors of the Apache-Mohaves stood up
to defend the lieutenant. Delche stopped laughing. He and
his men surrendered their weapons to the Yavapai police
and returned to their village under guard.

About the time Captain Burns and I left for Fort Whipple, Doctor Corbusier was on his way to the Rio Verde Indian Agency. When his wagon was within a few miles of the agency, forty or more Indians appeared in an open space where there were no rocks or trees to hide. The doctor and the driver took out their long-range, breechloading rifles and whipped the mules forward. Corbusier recognized the leader, and he believed that Delche recognized him. Neither party fired a shot.

The next day when Doctor Corbusier arrived at the Verde Agency, he had to care for many sick people. Doctor Williams and all his employees, most of Schuyler's men and nearly a thousand Yavapais were ill with fever. The white men and the Indians needed Doctor Corbusier's medicine and his help. He was just in time to save the other live Indians, but he was too late to save Delche. He and his warriors had escaped, and Sieber and his scouts were on their trail.

Six months later, Delche and his band were still hiding out in the hills and were blamed for raiding ranches around Prescott and for robbing and killing travelers on the roads. General Crook wanted him dead. When followers of Delche came to the agency asking for peace, Schuyler told them that they must first bring in Delche's head. Five days later while Schuyler was scouting in the Mazatzals, emissaries delivered Delche's scalp to Doctor Corbusier. The doctor recognized it at once to be the chief's scalp for hanging from the large ear of the dead Indian was the familiar pearl earring. That was the sad ending for the greatest chief of my people.

After Delche's death, the Yavapais lived peacefully on the Verde reservation, digging ditches, building brush dams and planting seeds. Soon they were harvesting all the food they needed. Because white men wanted the land that the Yavapais were working, all the Verde Indians were forced to move to San Carlos in February 1875. I think maybe

Delche had been right not to trust the white man's government.

About July 1875, the Fifth Cavalry was ordered to move back East. The Sixth Cavalry was coming to take its place. Lieutenant Hall S. Bishop, who had looked after me since Captain Burns had left with his family on sick leave, wrote General Crook asking permission to take me with him. The good hearted General Crook consented that I, "Apache Mickie"—that's the name he always called me—could go with the Fifth Cavalry. He told Bishop to see that he and his men took good care of me.

Officers' Quarters at Fort Whipple
Photo courtesy of Sharlot Hall Museum

17

Good-Bye to Arizona
and Old Friends
July — September 1875

I left Fort Whipple with Lieutenant Bishop and the men of
Company G on July 1, 1875. We took three days going to
Fort Verde where many men celebrated the Fourth of July
by getting drunk. When Lieutenant Bishop ordered an immediate departure, eight or ten troopers including my old
friend Sergeant Tom Handley were missing. They had deserted the troop. Lieutenant Bishop left without them. I
never knew why they quit the army and their friends in
Company G, but I later believed—after I had seen much of
the United States of America—that they probably liked the
Arizona climate better than any other climates.

That night the company camped at the headwaters of
Beaver Creek. We spent the whole next day moving the
wagons up to the water hole at the top of the hill. When the
command came to the divide, I went off by myself and
stood for a long time looking back toward the rolling hills
and streams of the Tonto Basin and Four Peaks. With wet
eyes I said good-bye to my homeland—to the water, the
trees and the rocks. I thought of my family and all the good
times. Tears poured down my face when I remembered all

the bad times and that I had no living relatives left in the land I was leaving. I howled out to the rocks and the hills, "I am moving away from my country to a strange place with strange people. There is a chance that I will not live to see the land of my people again."

I was very young, and my mood changed quickly. "I will be all right," I said to myself, "and 1 may yet live to return." I made up my mind to try to forget my people and the country I was leaving. But I could never forget all the things from my past, and sometimes I could not help feeling lonely when I was all alone in the big world.

At last we came to the Little Colorado River, which was very high and angry looking. Its swift waters carried thick red mud. After the difficult crossing, Company G camped on the other side. The next day we met the Sixth Cavalry heading for Fort Whipple. We traded our small Mexican horses, which could easily travel over rocks and rough mountains and live on weeds or brush and sunflowers, for larger horses from the Eastern states that were used to traveling on level plains.

We traveled a long hard day to make camp at Navajo Springs, a favorite watering place for travelers. Here we found a large meadow with good grass for the animals, but the water had a very strong odor and a bad taste. Skeletons of animals floated on the surface. I watched the company doctor approach the muddy springs. When he stepped on a place that appeared to be dry, he quickly sank into the mud clear to his shoulders. Many men rushed to his rescue, throwing him a rope and pulling on it until they finally got him out. The doctor was covered with mud so thick that a soldier scraped it off with a knife. His fine gold watch, which I had so admired, no longer looked very nice, and it soon stopped running.

The next day we came to a spring from which clear, cool water rushed out from under a large boulder, and it tasted like water. While we were drinking, many Navajos from a nearby village gathered around close to our campfire. In 1864 Colonel Kit Carson had driven the Navajos from their lands in northeastern Arizona to a reservation far away in southern New Mexico. The Navajos did not get along with the Apaches living there. Four years later after many had starved to death, they were allowed to return to their own country. They owned many sheep and goats that produced plenty of milk and provided the wool from which beautiful blankets were made. The Navajos came to trade blankets and cheese. Lieutenant Bishop bought some cheese for the company's supper.

I had never seen Navajos before, but they terrified me. I had often heard stories of these Indians capturing little children from other tribes and making them slaves. They spoke a language much like the White Mountain Apaches, and I could understand only a few words. When one Navajo spoke to me, I thought he asked who I was, but I was unable to tell him. Some soldiers teased me saying that these Navajos were going to take me to their camp and keep me there. So I ran to Lieutenant Bishop's tent where I slept each night and hid back in the corner. Lieutenant Bishop came to me laughing and asking why I was afraid. I did not say anything, for I feared the Indians might hear my voice and come in and drag me away. By evening the Indians left the camp, and I dared to leave my hiding place.

About that time Tom Broadwick came running into the camp, bareheaded and out of breath, shouting that Apaches were howling at him from the hills. He wanted the whole company to return to the place where he had heard many Apaches and where he had lost his hat. Tom was an old Irishman who could not read or write, but he was a jolly fellow. He told us about his frightening experience. Tom had set out to hunt rabbits; and as he strayed into a deep rocky canyon, he began to sing an old Irish song. Right away, he heard many strangers yelling back to him. He stopped; the voices stopped; but when he began to sing again, the strangers shouted back again. He thought that Apaches were in the hills and that when they saw him coming, they howled to each other. He became frightened and decided to retreat. In his haste he lost his hat. Often he stopped and looked back to see who was chasing him; he saw no one and he heard no more shouting.

A few soldiers went with Tom to the place where he had heard the Apaches yell at him. I, who had been brought up in rocky canyons, was not frightened and went along for the fun. Each time one of us spoke, we heard a noise from above. One soldier asked the old Irishman to sing again. His voice echoed from the rocky caves. The men laughed at him for behaving as a child.

After the command arrived at Fort Wingate, New Mexico, Lieutenant Bishop took me to the soldiers' graveyard, and we were shown where Captain Burns was laid to rest. When I saw the grave, I could not help shedding tears. When he was living, he treated me like his own child. I remembered his farewell words as he was taken to the wagon leaving Fort Whipple. "My boy," he said, "you will be all right. Soon after I return, we will depart for Ireland, to my father's home."

Several soldiers came to the grave. One soldier bowed his head and said a few words. The others fired their weapons several times over the grave. Lieutenant Bishop put his arm around me and said, "This is the way we say good-bye to our old friends."

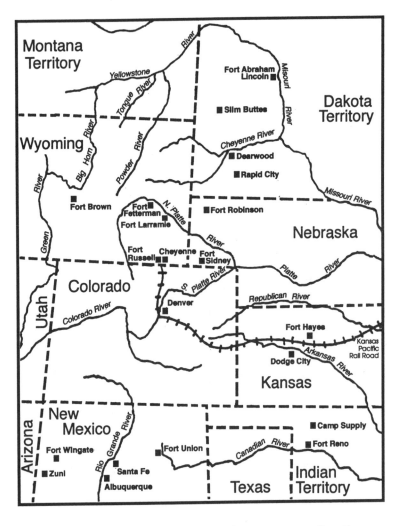

The Fifth Cavalry and the
Plains Indians
1875-1881

Part III

Mike, Lieutenant Bishop and The Plains Indians 1875 — 1881

18
Camp Supply, Indian Territory
September 1875 — May 1876

After companies from Fort Apache, Fort Thomas and the San Carlos Agency arrived at Fort Wingate, the Fifth Cavalry set out for Indian Territory. The first day we traveled through many Zuni pueblos. The Zunis have lived in these same villages for hundreds of years. For some reason the Spaniards thought the Zuni pueblos were the Seven Cities of Gold, and they stayed with these people for over one hundred years until the Zunis kicked them out. At one pueblo, Lieutenant Bishop bought five sheep for three dollars each, and the company ate fresh meat that night.

We could not ford the fast running waters of the Rio Grande, and it took all day to load all the wagons and horses on a ferry and for the Pueblo Indians to pull it to the other side. After camping just north of Albuquerque, we went on to Santa Fe and Fort Union where Captain Edward Hayes took over command of Company G. Lieutenant Bishop was now second in command.

At Fort Dodge, Kansas, General Wesley Merritt, who commanded all the Fifth Cavalry, ordered the companies to their stations. Some remained at Fort Dodge, but most of the companies went to someplace in Indian Territory. I was eager to ride on a train and envied the men going to Fort Riley who traveled by rail. Company G was ordered to Camp Supply, and we had to march overland ninety-five miles.

Most of the time, I rode with Lieutenant Bishop. We had some good conversations, and I enjoyed the scenery until we reached southern Kansas where I saw no more hills nor mountain ranges, only level plains covered mostly with buffalo grass, which is short, fine as feathers and a great feed for buffalo or cattle.

Three days out of Fort Dodge as we approached Camp Supply, light-colored animals appeared in the distance. I thought they were goats, but Bishop, who was looking through his field glasses, said, "We will have fresh antelope meat tonight."

Bishop got off his horse and handed me the bridle. He then went down on his knees and crawled until he was three or four hundred yards away from his target. He raised his gun and fired twice at the animals. Neither antelope fell. One galloped over the plain away from us, but the other limped away weakly. As I rode over to Bishop, he shouted, "I hit one. It looks almost dead. Let's ride quickly and overtake the wounded animal." He got on his horse and went on a run. I could not keep up with Lieutenant Bishop who had the faster horse and was soon close to the wounded antelope. I was riding down hill and did not hold the reins because I was holding my heavy gun with both hands, watching and ready to shoot if an antelope turned toward me.

Suddenly, the horse I rode stumbled and went down on his back. I fell to the side of the horse with one leg caught under the saddle. The horse rolled over me. I yelled so loudly that Bishop heard me and saw the four hoofs rising in the air. He quickly got to where I was lying under the horse and pulled the bridle to one side so that my horse would roll over. When Bishop had freed my legs, he took me by the arms to help me stand up, but I could not stand. One leg was broken. The horse was not hurt in any way, only the saddle and myself. Lieutenant Bishop told me to remain there. Soon he was back with a light wagon and two men who laid me on a blanket and carried me to the wagon. A soldier rode my horse without a saddle.

Luckily for me, there was a good doctor at Camp Supply who could set my leg and put it in a cast, and no one had to cut it off. After a few weeks in the hospital, I was as good as new and went back to stay with Lieutenant Bishop. The doctor was very kind to me, and Lieutenant Bishop and my friends from Company G visited me as often as they could. But it was very hard for me, who was only about ten years old at the time, to remain so idle and careful so my leg would heal right.

I was very curious about every place and every thing I saw. While I was in the hospital waiting for my leg to mend, I asked a lot of questions about many things. The doctors and visitors answered my questions as best they could. I often asked, "What is Indian Territory?" Someone always said, "It is a big reservation where many different Indian tribes live." When I returned to Indian Territory several years later, I talked to Indians who lived there. Then I learned all about the place.

When the white men wanted all the Eastern Indians' land for themselves, the United States government decided to make this part of their large country "Indian Territory"— now called Oklahoma—a place where they could put many Indian tribes. Before all kinds of Indians moved to Indian Territory, the eastern part was home to the Osages and Quapaws. The Wichitas, Caddoes, Comanches, Kiowas and Plains Apaches lived in the western lands. The government made treaties with the Osages and the Quapaws who agreed to give up their lands, but the other tribes signed no treaties.

The white men wanted the good farm lands of the Cherokees, Chocktows, Creeks, Seminoles and Chicksaws in Georgia, Florida, Alabama and Mississippi. Their story is much like the story of my people, the Yavapais, except that these five tribes were not so wild. They were called The Five Civilized Tribes. Many were educated—even better educated than many white men who stole their land. They dressed like white men, lived in big houses on big farms, built schools and Christian churches, and some even owned black slaves.

In the 1830s the government forced these Five Civilized Tribes—Cherokees, Chocktaws, Creeks, Seminoles and Chicksaws—to give up their lands in the Southeast and move to lands in Indian Territory. These Indians suffered on their western journey. About one-fourth of the people died from hardship and diseases on the way. The Indians called this march the "Trail of Tears."

The Five Civilized Tribes made a new life in the wilds of Indian Territory. They made new governments and built new ranches and towns. In the western part of the territory, the Wichitas and Caddoes were peaceful farmers who raised corn, beans, pumpkins, melons and squash and lived in dome-shaped houses covered with grass. Many spoke English and traded with the Americans.

But the Plains Indians—Comanches, Kiowas and Plains Apaches—were like the wild Apaches of Arizona. They did no farming but got their food by hunting buffalo and raiding settlements as far south as Mexico. The Plains Indians did not want strangers coming to their lands, and their fierce warriors attacked travelers on the roads. When the government decided to settle these tribes on a new reservation in Indian Territory, they refused to go there. Because the war broke out in the East, the government could not make them settle on the reservation.

In 1861 the Indians of Indian Territory were well off. During the war, the Southern and Northern armies fought many battles there. By the time the war was over, most farms and towns had been burned, and many people had died. After the war, the government took much land away from the Five Civilized Tribes and forced the Plains Indians on reservations. White settlers and Indians from many tribes moved into Indian Territory. Camp Supply was built in 1868 to protect peaceful white men and Indians from the Plains Indians, especially the Cheyennes and Arapahos, and sometimes against disobedient bands from other tribes.

Many prairie chickens, wild turkeys and buffalo roamed about in that prairie country around Fort Supply. Men from Company G went out on wagons for three or four days to Beaver Creek and the Canadian River and returned with several turkeys and buffalo meat. Lieutenant Bishop let me go two or three miles down the river banks to hunt. One night, I borrowed a shot gun and shells and strolled along the river until I reached a thick growth of trees. It was getting dark and there was no moon, but I could hear turkeys gobbling. As I crept up to a large cottonwood, I spied two large turkeys. I blasted away at them, and they fell to the ground. I put them in a large sack, threw the sack over my shoulder, and trudged homeward.

I was so proud of being a great hunter and knew that the officers in the mess I shared would be pleased to feast on the fine birds. But by the time I reached the kitchen, I felt so tired from carrying the heavy birds, I just opened the door and tossed the sack on the floor.

The next morning, I was so hungry for turkey, I jumped out of bed, dressed quickly and ran to the mess. When I did not smell them cooking, I asked the cook if he had seen the bundle with two turkeys. The cook was not in a good humor and answered angrily, "Take those stinking buzzards away from here. Buzzards are not fit to eat." As I went out the back door, I saw the sack laying on the ground away from the building. In the dark I had mistaken the buzzards for turkeys and had trekked nearly five miles carrying the big shot gun and the heavy sack—all for nothing.

One night about midnight, in late January 1876, Lieutenant Bishop woke me and said to get ready for a march. Cattlemen had come into Camp Supply and reported to the commanding officer that Osage Indians had driven their cattle off to the north, burning the prairie behind them. Many years before the white men came and all the United States was Indian country, the Osage Indians lived in lands east of the Mississippi. When the white men saw the Osage land, they made the Osages trade it for a reservation in Kansas. Soon white men wanted the Kansas land, the government bought it, and the Osages moved to Indian Territory. Sometimes the Osages made trouble for the white ranchers.

Captain Emil Adam, ordered Lieutenant Bishop to try to recapture the stolen cattle. A trooper brought us two horses, each with a gun and cartridges strapped to the saddle. Lieutenant Bishop, about fifty soldiers, two cowboys, and one Indian boy—me—marched down the Canadian River about twenty-five miles and arrived at the cattle ranch where we camped until morning. At day break, three more cowboys joined us for breakfast. After the cowboys showed us where the Indians had driven off the animals, we followed the trail that the Indians and cattle had made. A little farther down the trail, we found the remains of three dead animals. The Indians had taken only the best parts and set fire to the rest. Almost one hundred head of cattle made a great path, but much of the trail had been burned and was difficult in places to follow.

For three days we followed the thieves' trail along the Seminole River seeing nothing but remains of dead cattle and much smoke on the other side of the river. When we found a place to ford the river, we crossed and camped for the night. The next morning, we found the tall prairie grass burned, and the trail had disappeared. Bishop ordered us to hurry out of the scorched land and find the trail again. Sure enough, when we reached the end, we saw cattle and horse tracks and places where the Indians had killed more animals. We could not tell how many because the Indians had taken all the parts. We soon discovered several trails with one trail wider than the others, and we knew then that the Indians had separated into smaller groups and that one group had taken most of the herd.

We camped for the night on a little creek. The next morning, Lieutenant Bishop said that we must be near the thieves' village and to prepare for a fight. After riding about ten miles, through fog so thick I could not see the man ahead of me, we suddenly came upon several ponies. We had arrived at the edge of an Indian camp without even knowing it. Also, because the morning was so dark with fog, the Indians did not know we were there either. Speaking in a low voice, Lieutenant Bishop told me and some soldiers to stay with the horses, but he ordered the others to dismount and attack. Lieutenant Bishop thought I was too young to stand the fight, that I was better off guarding the horses. In a few minutes we heard shots, but we could not tell if the soldiers or Indians had fired first. We had a hard time keeping the horses we were guarding from running off. The bullets whistled over our heads, but we dodged them by hiding our heads in the sides of the horses.

At the village, the soldiers captured thirty-seven women and children and many ponies. Three Indians—one chief and two warriors—and one soldier had died. The other Indian warriors ran off to get more Indians. Although we could see more tepees beyond the camp, we did not continue the scout. Bishop feared we might come upon a great many Indians and ordered his men to be quick about putting the prisoners on ponies without saddles and race back toward Camp Supply. If we had not made a run for it, the same thing might have happened to us as what later happened to General George Custer.

With gun in hand, I was part of the gang guarding and driving the captured Indian ponies. Because of the heavy fog, we could see only the animals right next to us. We rode about thirty-five miles back to the Seminole River and made camp among the many cottonwoods.

Lieutenant Bishop gave orders not to build fires that night and told us to have our guns ready for action at any notice. Some prisoners had told a cowboy that over one hundred fifty Indians would come to the camp to rescue them and their animals. The captives were kept near the ponies and guarded all night. I hid with two soldiers between two big cottonwood logs that had fallen close together. But I could not sleep the whole night. Two old women sang and howled loudly until morning, and I feared the young men might hear them and attack us during the night. Some soldiers got very angry and wanted to shoot the women, but Lieutenant Bishop said not to do anything of the sort until other enemies showed up. Then they could do as they pleased.

The sons of our captives must not have heard their howling because the expected attack never happened, and in the morning light we counted two hundred fifty ponies. However, as we rode up the east side of the Seminole River, fifteen soldiers stayed back about one-half mile to watch for the enemy. After crossing the Seminole River, we made camp, and Bishop ordered twenty-five men to be on guard all night. The next morning, my heart became more contented as we met twenty-five to thirty soldiers who joined us in a safe trip back to Camp Supply.

As we approached the camp, I showed Lieutenant Bishop two ponies that I liked in the captured herd. He said I could get them after we arrived in camp. But after we got the prisoners and the ponies in the hands of the military authorities, we learned that Captain Emil Adam had received orders from General Sheridan that the prisoners and the ponies were to be escorted back to their homes at the Darlington Agency near Fort Reno. The commanding officer was to see that nothing was taken away from these Indians. All I wanted for my service and risking my life were two pretty ponies, but Bishop said that we had to give up the ponies and that we were going to take them to Fort Reno with the captives.

Early in May 1876, Captain Adam received orders from the Department Commander, that all the Fifth Cavalry, which was scattered over the boundless prairies of Kansas and Oklahoma, was to join General Crook. All companies were to head without delay to the nearest railroad station, which in our case was at Fort Dodge, and then to Fort Russell near Cheyenne, Wyoming. General Crook was out near the Big Horn Mountains fighting the Sioux Indians who were away from their reservations and on the warpath. When General Crook could not do much with the soldiers he had in his command, he thought about the Fifth Cavalry that had fought with him in Arizona against the wild Apaches and against my people who were not so wild. In Arizona he became known as a great Indian fighter.

Company G had become like my family. When I heard the news about the troops leaving Camp Supply, I feared that I would be left behind alone without a friend. But Lieutenant Bishop, who was a close friend and like a father to me, said we must go together.

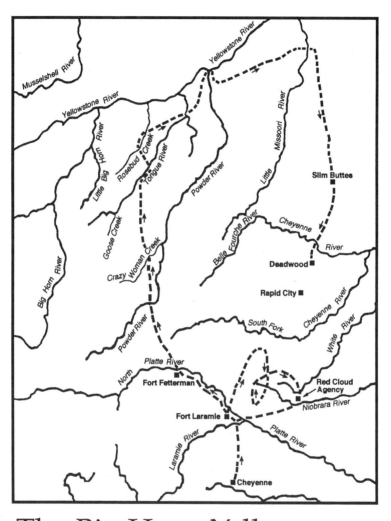

The Big Horn-Yellowstone
Campaign 1876

19

Trains, Wagons, Chewing Tobacco and Buffalo Bill
June 6 – 21, 1876

At Dodge City, Kansas, the soldiers loaded all the horses, the company property and the mess outfits in the railroad cars. They next placed the saddles on top of the cars keeping them in place by fastening the one saddle strap to the next, and stacking the blankets between them. Finally, all the officers and men and scouts and servants boarded the train. The Kansas-Pacific headed north toward Denver and Cheyenne. I was very excited and also rather scared. I was taking the first railroad ride of my life.

I joined the men sitting on top of the cars. They were having a great time shooting at antelope and buffalo, but all their bullets struck the ground and never hit an animal. I was always eager to shoot at something. So I took my old Henry rifle and started firing, and all my bullets hit ahead of the antelope. The Fifth Cavalry had to get to Cheyenne quickly, so we traveled much faster than the passengers on an ordinary train. After they grew tired of shooting and not hitting anything, some men went back into the cars.

I enjoyed the scenery on the Colorado plains, for far ahead I could see the mountains again, and I remained on top. I saw soldiers fastening a saddle strap to one wrist—for what reason I did not know and I did not ask—but I did the same. For a long time, I watched the snow covered Pike's Peak until the rocking motion of the train put me to sleep. I woke suddenly and found myself at the rim of the car with half my body hanging over the side at the end of the strap. When I remembered where I was, I grabbed hold of another strap and crawled up to the top of the car, stood on my feet and breathed a new life. That strap fastened tightly to my wrist saved me. If I had not tied that strap to my wrist before going to sleep, I would have slid over the car and under the wheels and been all mashed up. The great Omniscient was at hand and gave me a new chance at life.

Finally, the train with the soldiers and the horses and the properties arrived at Cheyenne, Wyoming Territory. We did not stay there long but moved right on to Fort Russell just a few miles away. There on another broad prairie, the command waited for recruits and new horses. Soon other companies of the Fifth Cavalry arrived with many recruits on the Union Pacific increasing each company to about eighty-five men. Here Buffalo Bill Cody and his close companion Buffalo Chips joined us as scouts.

Many cavalry officers knew Bill Cody well, and they greeted him as a long-lost friend. He had been the chief scout of the Fifth Cavalry for three years on the plains until he decided to have a career in the theater. Cody was putting on a big show in a city in the East when he read in the papers that the Fifth was ordered to join General Crook. He rushed through his performance, got on the midnight express, and four days later arrived in Cheyenne. Bishop told me that throughout the cavalry Chief Scout Cody was better known than any general except Crook. He was a great hero as a scout as well as an actor. I was very proud to meet the famous Buffalo Bill.

With Cody was his friend since boyhood and faithful follower Buffalo Chips. His real name was James White. He copied Cody in every way he could. They wore their long hair the same way—Bill's hair was brown and Chip's yellow—and they wore the same kind of clothes. I got to know him over the next few weeks. He was the best-mannered scout I ever met. Not once—and the Fifth went through some pretty rough times before he died—did I hear Chips swear or see him drink wine or whiskey.

General Wesley Merritt and ten Fifth Cavalry troops received orders to go on to Fort Laramie. Few horses arrived, and I had none to ride. Lieutenant Bishop received permission for me to ride in one of the lightly loaded grain wagons. I crawled into the covered wagon and lay between two sacks of grain. I rode this way for several miles wishing I could see the scenery. I could not look out because the wagon was covered with thick canvas and was fastened at both ends. All at once, I felt the wagon roll rapidly downward, and I heard a kind of cracking sound as it went over into a deep gulch. I screamed for help. The sacks of grain piled on top of me. The soldiers guarding the wagons rushed to my rescue. They could not untie the strings that held down the cover. I gasped for breath as they cut the canvas sheets to get me out. Finally, someone got hold of my little hands and pulled on me, but the many grain sacks on top of me held my body tight. The soldiers had to take the sacks off me one at a time until I could free myself. I found nothing much injured. It might have been hard luck for me if I had not fallen flat on my stomach.

Many men in the command besides me had no horses. While we waited at Fort Laramie for new horses to arrive, we received bad news about General George Crook. All the trouble began when white prospectors found gold in the Big

Horn Mountains. Just like in Arizona, the white men wanted the Indians' best land for themselves, and the Sioux and Cheyennes did not want to give it to them. General Crook and over one thousand soldiers went into the Big Horn Mountain country to make the Sioux and Cheyennes go to the Red Cloud Reservation in Nebraska. Too many Sioux waited for him. On June 17 at Rosebud Creek, Chief Crazy Horse forced General Crook to retreat. The Sioux killed over a dozen men and wounded many more. This Battle of the Rosebud was the only time the Indians beat General Crook. I often wondered what might have happened if the Fifth Cavalry had been there to help him.

The regiment headed north to join General Crook in the Big Horn Mountains. I was so happy to have a horse of my own again. But even riding a horse became tiring and boring after many hours. I suffered from the weather, sometimes the heat and sometimes the cold, and I was often hungry or thirsty. As I rode along side a soldier in Company G, we talked about the hardships of scouting expeditions. The soldier said that tobacco, especially chewing tobacco, always helped keep him from feeling hungry or thirsty and made him feel strong. Then he handed me a piece of tobacco, saying it was his last chew. I quickly accepted it and put it in my mouth. At the first taste, I wanted to spit it out, but I was afraid the soldier would be angry and scold me. We were in wild country with no places to get more tobacco. I kept the tobacco in my mouth for at least two hours before I finally spit it out. The tobacco taste was so strong that I could not speak and only motioned for water. I did not drink the water but tried to wash my mouth out with it. I did not dare to drink much water as we were traveling over unknown country and did not know where or when we might come to the next water supply.

I talked to nobody. When we reached camp, I rode up to Lieutenant Bishop, but I could not get off the horse in the usual manner. When I rolled off to the ground, Lieutenant Bishop asked who had given me whiskey. I just shook my head. He thought I was drunk and had someone unsaddle my horse while he spread a blanket for me to lie down. I just lay there until evening. When supper was ready, Bishop asked me to get up and eat. But I did not care to eat anything yet. He laughed and went on with his supper. I vomited all through the night. The next morning, I still did not care to eat. Lieutenant Bishop thought I should go to the doctor for some medicine. I then told him about the tobacco. I said that my sickness was my own fault and that I would be well in a few days. I learned the hard way that tobacco did not make scouting easier.

The command marched down the Laramie River where we camped for the night. The next day while we camped at Sage Creek, General Merritt received a telegram from the headquarters in Omaha, by way of Fort Laramie. Hundreds of Cheyennes had fled the Red Cloud Reservation and were going north to join Sitting Bull and Crazy Horse in the Big Horn Mountains. We were to cut off these Indians. General Merritt hoped we could find them before they found us.

Early the next morning, we moved out to Crazy Woman's Fork and made camp on Milk Creek where the little running water was so thick with a whitish clay mud that it looked like milk. It did not taste like milk, and it did not taste like water either. Even the horses would not drink it. There was no other water. To make coffee, the soldiers dug down over fifteen feet to find good water. The next day, the command camped among some cottonwood trees near a stream of clear water.

We were now in hostile Indian country. Each company went out in a different direction to find the enemy. Every time we camped, a man was sent out with a signal flag. Some flags had a white square in the center; others had a black square. One sentinel signaled down to camp that about thirty Indians were heading from the east toward the camp. Foolishly, the guard stood right in the sight of the Indians who could see the flag with a white square moving. The Indians could understand its warning, and they hurriedly retreated in the direction of the Red Cloud Agency and safety.

Soldiers and scouts soon hurried out after the fleeing Indians. That night, the men and horses returned all tired out without a sign of Cheyennes. The next day while the command remained in camp, scouts led by Buffalo Bill Cody went toward the Black Hills to check for Indian trails heading north toward the Big Horn or southeast toward the Red Cloud Agency. When the scouts returned, they reported that they saw no signs of Indians going north or toward the agency. Cody said that if any Indians were around, they knew where the Fifth Cavalry was and avoided us.

We camped at Sage Creek waiting for a courier to return from Laramie, seventy miles away. When a lieutenant arrived from Fort Robinson with a message for General Merritt, he called all the officers together. After the meeting, everyone looked so unhappy, and some officers had tears in their eyes. Later, Bishop told me the sad news. The news about General George Armstrong Custer was bad—at least for the army, especially for the Seventh Cavalry. It was good news for the Sioux. One week after Crook's retreat from the Rosebud, Custer and five cavalry companies attacked a Sioux village in the foothills of the Big Horn Mountains. He did not know that Chief Crazy Horse and fifteen hundred Sioux warriors were waiting for them. Custer and two hundred twenty-five officers and men were wiped out. No one survived. No wonder, Lieutenant Bishop looked so sad. Many of his West Point friends and classmates died in that battle.

Merritt's command was ordered to head north without delay to join General Crook's command on Goose Creek.

Five days later, when we were about a one-day march from Fort Laramie, Merritt received a message from the Red. Cloud Reservation that nearly a thousand Cheyennes were preparing to escape. They had probably heard about the Sioux's success at Little Big Horn Mountain and hoped to join Chief Crazy Horse there. So we turned back in the direction from which we had just come and headed toward the Red Cloud Agency.

We camped that night at Sage Creek, and the next day we set up camp at Cottonwood Flats near War Bonnet Creek. Most of the command stayed in camp that day while Buffalo Bill and Buffalo Chips and a dozen scouts set out to search the hilly countryside, which was full of deep canyons. About a half hour later, the sentry signaled to us that two horsemen were coming over the trail about three miles from camp. A few moments later, Cody spied Indians on the opposite side of the hill where the scouts and soldiers watched. The Indians were creeping up on the two horsemen, whom Cody now believed to be soldiers, as they approached a deep canyon.

Buffalo Bill feared the Indians would soon ambush the two men and within seconds could kill or capture and torture them. He also feared he was too far away to save them. Five mounted Indians and three on foot climbed close to the edge of the canyon. One Indian wore a great feathered war bonnet.

Buffalo Bill, who was an expert shot, decided that the only way out of the dangerous situation was to fire with his long-range fifty-caliber rifle. So Cody aimed his rifle at the chief who was nearly a mile away and fired. When the smoke cleared, the scouts noticed that the chief's horse had fallen. With the next shot Cody's bullet hit the chief. When Buffalo Bill and Buffalo Chips got to where the dead Indian lay, they recognized him as Yellow Hand, a young Cheyenne chief from the Red Cloud Agency. Buffalo Bill Cody fired just in time to save the soldiers who were bringing a message to General Merritt.

I was usually with the rear guard of the command and often did not see much fighting. But when we heard the sound of Buffalo Bill's shot, I rushed with the rest of the men to the place where Chief Yellow Hand and his horse lay dead. From the crest of the hill, we saw below us—about two miles away—hundreds of Indians scattering right and left over the rolling prairie and all heading toward the reservation. When the soldiers caught up with the Cheyenne army, they chased it back to the Red Cloud Reservation. About noon we set up camp just outside the agency at Fort Robinson. We had nothing to eat, but we slept well that night. The Fifth Cavalry had kept these Cheyennes from joining Sitting Bull in the Big Horn Mountains.

The next morning General Merritt was in a big hurry to get going. The men saved by Buffalo Bill had brought orders from General Sheridan that the Fifth Cavalry was to waste no more time in joining General Crook at Goose Creek. There was just one problem. I was hungry. Everyone in the command was hungry. No one had eaten a thing since breakfast the day before. We had all rushed off chasing the Cheyennes without food or mess kits, and the quartermaster wagons lagged far behind. General Merritt was about to send someone to the agency to see about rations when luckily for us—and for the reservation Indians who might have gone without food for a while—the quartermaster, Lieutenant Hall, drove up with the wagon train of supplies. Two hours later, after eating a good breakfast, we began our more than three hundred mile trek to Goose Creek.

20
Off to the Big Horn
July 21 — August 6, 1876

A two day march from Fort Robinson brought us to Fort Laramie where we camped for the night, picked up more supplies and were on our way up the North Platte River. The trip was boring, the scenery all the same—only flat plains as far as I could see, and the weather was not nice. The hot, burning rays of the summer sun and the dust blowing into our faces made riding uncomfortable. The soldiers suffered more than I did. Because I was born in a hot place, I was used to such weather. In Arizona the Fifth Cavalry campaigned mostly in winter, and the troops usually marched at night.

Early in the afternoon of the third day, we stopped for a brief rest. Many officers and men stripped to their underwear and cooled off in the river, and I did the same. Right after we were on our way again, a very strong wind with hailstones came upon us. The cold rain beat upon our tent all night long and followed us all the way to Fort Fetterman. At Laramie we were joined by many wagons, new horses, more officers and soldiers, and the medical director of the expedition, Doctor Clements.

The next day, we met two frightened and tired prospectors coming on foot from the mountains. They said that four days earlier, while they camped with five others near the Powder River, about seventy-five Indians had attacked and killed their companions. Merritt sent three companies under Major John Upham to escort the two surviving prospectors to the scene of the massacre, to bury the dead, and to catch up with the main command at the Powder River Crossing. The rest of us moved north toward the Powder River.

For three days we marched across the endless plains under a scorching sun. We saw no grass or trees, only white, dusty ground and sagebrush. As we trudged wearily along, I looked far ahead to the Big Horn Mountains, their snow-covered peaks sparkling in the bright sunshine. Lieutenant Bishop said the peaks were more than fifty miles away.

As we prepared to camp on the Powder River, its water thick with gray dirt and not fit to drink, we heard cavalry trumpets in the distance. Our trumpeters answered back. Soon Companies E and F joined us. Now General Merritt commanded ten companies of the Fifth Cavalry.

Twenty miles from the Big Horn, we camped on the banks of Crazy Woman's Fork. The cool breezes coming down from the mountains felt so good. Upham's companies had not joined us on time. Merritt was worried so he sent two companies to look for them. While we waited, nearly every man in the command wanted to scout the country and shoot Indians. General Merritt warned them that they would soon have enough scouting and enough shooting. Finally, Upham's lost command and the two prospectors appeared. The prospectors stayed with us hoping to find the Indians who had killed their comrades.

The next morning we rode through a hilly country where we saw several small herds of buffalo. I had not seen the big shaggy animals since my train ride from Fort Dodge to Cheyenne. Buffalo Bill and a few officers chased after them. I felt unhappy because I was not allowed to join in the hunt. Early in the afternoon, we stopped at Clear Fork to have lunch and drink the cool water that came from the snow-covered mountains. We rested until five and trekked into the foothills to make camp.

We woke to the sight of a high mountain ridge from which rose the headwaters of the Tongue, the Rosebud and the Big Horn Rivers. Lieutenant Bishop told me that somewhere on the other side of that ridge, Crook and his men were waiting for us to join them. I also learned from listening to talk among the men that somewhere between us and Crook, ten thousand Sioux, Northern Cheyennes and their allies might be waiting to wipe us out.

Traveling became very slow and difficult, especially for the wagons. I was happy that Company G did not have to stay behind with the wagon train that day, because the guards would be the last to reach the top of the ridge. The road ran up and down over hills and through deep gorges. We passed the ruins of abandoned old Fort Phil Kearney and watered our horses at a clear stream that flowed northeast to where it emptied into the Yellowstone. I thought we would camp there, but we stopped only to rest and eat lunch and continued on until we reached the top.

From the top we saw that the whole country to the north was black with smoke. Just to disappoint us and prevent our animals from eating the grass, Sitting Bull's Indians had set fire to the country they wanted. Early in the afternoon we stopped along another cool, clear stream where many brightly colored trout were swimming. We did not stay long enough to catch any. Late that night while we were making camp, a messenger brought news from General Crook. We were only fifteen miles from his camp.

We were not allowed much sleep, and before the sun came up, the bugle call was sounded for the first time since leaving Fort Fetterman. General Merritt feared the enemy might hear it. The companies hurried to get breakfast. When our command was about two miles from General Crook's main camp, two Second Cavalry companies, with the general at the head of the column, met us. We followed Crook down a long, steep hill to his camp near Goose Creek.

At that time I could not know for sure what day of the month it was, nor the name of the month either, because I was not educated in those days. And you must remember that I had spent only four years in civilization. I understood the English language well enough to get along, but I could not read or write. I know now that we met General Crook's command on August 6, fifty-six days after the Rosebud fight. Merritt arrived with ten companies of the Fifth Cavalry—a total of over eight hundred fifty men. I supposed that I was not counted, but Lieutenant Bishop said that he would make sure I was carried on as a volunteer Indian Scout of the Fifth United States Cavalry so I would have a horse and rations.

Crook's command was even larger than ours with ten companies of the Second and Third Cavalry, two infantry companies, an artillery platoon, one hundred fifty white and Indian scouts, packers and teamsters, miners, and other civilians totaling about twelve hundred men. More than three hundred Shoshones under Washakie and Arapahos under Aligator-Stand-Up had recently been brought into camp by Chief of Scouts Frank Gruard and joined Crooks' campaign against their enemies the Cheyennes and Sioux. The whole campaign now numbered about twenty-three hundred men and one hundred sixty wagons.

General Crook wanted to catch the escaping Indians; so he decided to leave ten men from each company behind with the slow-moving wagons. Each officer and soldier could take only necessary things like an overcoat, blankets, mess items and ammunition. Pack mules carried extra rations and ammunition.

I must not forget to tell you of my meeting with General George Crook. One evening, right after supper, Lieutenant Bishop took me to the general's tent located among the willow and cottonwood trees. It was fully three long years since we had last seen him. Lieutenant Bishop and I were poor examples of soldiers. We looked rather ragged and poor after having spent seven weeks chasing wild Indians. We had marched over eight hundred miles since we had left Cheyenne. Our jackets and trousers were worn and tattered, and I had nearly outgrown all my clothes. General Crook looked almost as poor as I did. He wore a worn shooting jacket, slouch felt hat, and soldier's boots, and his long scraggly beard was tied into braids.

He recognized me as soon as he saw me with Lieutenant Bishop. His eyes twinkled and he took both my hands. "Well, well!" he said, "Here is the Apache boy Mickie Burns. You have grown. How are you Mickie? Are you not lost being so far away from your home?" General Crook thought my people were some tribe of Apaches.

I said, "I have no home. My home is just where I make my bed, sir."

I think he was surprised that I now spoke such good English. "That is true, my boy. I forgot about all your family being killed in the Salt River Cave," he said. "It had to be done, or there would still be killing and you would not be alive today. My boy, Mickie, forget all about the past and resolve to do the best you can by yourself. You will be a great soldier when you are old enough. Just listen to Bishop's advice. He will never lead you wrong."

21
Where Did all the Sioux Go?
August 8 — September 6, 1876

General George Crook's Big Horn and Yellowstone expe-
dition began two days after the Fifth Cavalry's arrival at
Goose Creek. The column stretched out for two miles; the
Shoshones were in the lead eager to take on the enemy; the
Fifth Cavalry was in the rear. We followed Prairie Dog
Creek toward its junction with the Tongue River. General
Crook's Indian scouts had reported the Sioux and Cheyenne
moving northeast toward the Tongue River.

The first days out were clear and cloudless. We stopped
often, whenever we came upon buffalo grass, to let the
horses graze. We feared that up ahead where clouds of
smoke rose high above the mountains there might be no
grass. About noon we came upon the rushing Tongue River.
At least twenty times during the next two days we had to
ford the winding stream. The water came up over my shoulders, and I was glad that my horse could carry me across. I
was thankful that I was a cavalry scout and not in the infantry. Each time an infantry man crossed, he had to remove
his shoes, stockings and trousers.

At night when we rolled up in our blankets and slept
on the ground using our saddles for pillows, we were
thankful for the clear skies. We had no tents and no beds,

only one bed blanket and a rubber blanket each. I was very tired and slept soundly. We shivered in the cool morning air, but the steaming coffee soon warmed us. All the time we marched we wondered when we would come upon the Sioux. The smoke clouds drifting against the distant mountains told us that Red Cloud was not far ahead.

When we reached the summit of the divide between the Tongue and the Rosebud Rivers, we saw the Rosebud about six or eight miles below and knew that somewhere down there Crook had lost his big fight with Crazy Horse. We took three hours to reach the valley. The Sioux had burned every blade of grass, and they had left many other signs behind. Sergeant Lynch, who had fought against Indians for many years, declared that the whole Sioux nation had camped there about two weeks earlier. Another old timer said that they were not more than four days ahead. We continued on the trail of nearly ten thousand Indians.

With the Fifth Cavalry leading the column, we rode all night. There was no moonlight, so we went down Rosebud Creek in total darkness. Often I gripped my saddle for fear I would fall off my horse. Sometimes I would sleep, but the horses' noises soon woke me. No man dared speak or light a match to smoke on a night march. We followed each other so closely that sometimes the horses would knock hooves. I was very tired and about to fall off my house when someone whispered, "Make a rest stop, but do not unsaddle your horses."

We rested about two hours until daylight and marched on again—without breakfast—following the Rosebud to within thirty miles of the Yellowstone River. As we rode along we could see great clouds of dust beyond a hill about a mile away. I thought we would soon be in the midst of a big fight, and I was very frightened.

Bishop peered through his field glasses and laughed. "Stop shaking, Mike," he said, "I see soldiers, not Indians.

We are not facing the Sioux Nation but General Terry and the Seventh Cavalry."

Here on August 11, we met General Alfred Terry's command coming up from steamboats on the Yellowstone River. With him were two infantry regiments and what remained of the Seventh Cavalry. Everyone asked, "Where are the Sioux?"

The Fifth Infantry commanded by General Nelson Miles did not stick around long enough for Lieutenant Bishop to greet his classmates. General Miles marched north looking for bands of Sioux that might be headed for Canada.

After Crazy Horse beat General Custer at Little Big Horn, General Terry's command had withdrawn to the Yellowstone to wait for new orders and more recruits. When he started south down the valley of the Yellowstone, Terry, like Crook, expected to meet a lot of Indians at every turn. Terry and his command were as surprised to see us as we were to see them.

However, unlike us, Terry traveled with a complete wagon train with tents and plenty of equipment. We had only our blankets, a few day's supply of bacon, hardtack, coffee and sugar and as much ammunition as when we had left Goose Creek. General Terry and his officers and soldiers looked like the ones you see in photographs. In General Crook's command, unless you knew them, you could not tell the officers from the men. Everyone in the Fifth Cavalry wore worn-out Arizona scouting outfits of buckskin, flannel or corduroy, and we had no change of clothing with us.

The next morning, we loaded our mules with rations from General Terry's wagon and continued chasing the enemy. General Terry's command led the way. The whole force including the Indian allies now totaled about four thousand men. We marched rapidly eastward, passed over a mountain range for eight to ten miles, pushed on through a canyon and down a hill, and camped near the Tongue River.

Dark clouds that had gathered all day sprinkled us lightly in the afternoon. About sunset the rains poured down upon us. Some of the men tried to build huts—like my people did—of saplings and twigs and threw ponchos and blankets over them. They wasted their time; the rain came pouring through. No one could sleep so we huddled around fires in the squishy mud until the next afternoon.

For the next several days, we followed an Indian trail east across a muddy plain between the Tongue and the Yellowstone. Whenever the rain quit, we tried to squeeze the water out of our soaked blankets. It was no use because the rain soon poured down upon us again, each time colder than the time before. The horses did not seem to mind the rain. Despite the fires of the Sioux, they found plenty of grass, but these horses were used to eating grain and started to wear out. The men were tired too, and many became sick. Our rations were soaked. We had only salt meat and hardtack to eat. I was not sick, only cold and hungry.

Late in the evening, on August 15, we reached the Powder River. We followed the river north and camped near a ridge overlooking the Yellowstone. The officers in the headquarters camped by the only trees around. The rest of us camped on the sandy shore where there were no trees or bluffs or anything to protect us from the strong winds.

For three days, we enjoyed nice weather as we waited for the supply ship to come in. The soldiers had a great time fishing and hunting while Sitting Bull—the Indian chief we were after—was escaping to Canada. The Crows and the Shoshones became disgusted with the lack of action in the campaign and returned home to their families.

The heavy rains returned, and the winds became fierce. Because we had no shelter we could not sleep. Everyone gathered around the big fires. My very best friend Lieutenant Bishop became ill. When I noticed his blankets lying in the mud, I gathered brush and grass to put under his bedding, moved him closer to the fire, and ran for the doctor. He attended Bishop daily, and he was soon all right again.

The supply ship, the Far West, arrived from Omaha with much needed rations. All the injured and sick were carried aboard. By this time Lieutenant Bishop was almost completely well and did not have to leave me. Our best scout, Buffalo Bill Cody, returned to Omaha on the boat, and from there he headed East by train to continue his drama career. Jonathan White, better known as Buffalo Chips and until now Bill Cody's inseparable partner, continued to scout for Crook. As things turned out, Buffalo Chips should have gone with his friend.

After remaining on the Yellowstone River for seven days, we marched up the Powder still looking for the Indians who had gone south. Almost everyone in the Fifth Cavalry walked because the horses were in such bad shape. The supply ship from Omaha had not brought enough oats for them. On August 25, couriers from General Sheridan brought new orders, and the next day the two commands separated. General Terry hurried back to the Yellowstone to guard its crossings. Crook followed the trail of the Sioux southeast toward the Black Hills.

Before leaving camp, General Crook ordered all his commanders to tell their men that they must not shoot their guns. We could kill anything we wanted but not with bullets. The next day before reaching our camp, we saw many prairie chickens—some as large as the tame chickens I had cared for at Camp Date Creek. The soldiers killed them with clubs and we roasted them that night.

Two days later as we marched through the rolling prairies near the Little Missouri River valley, we came upon some structures that reminded me of the shades of my people. Whoever built them had spread sticks, brush and blankets over four posts made from slender tree trunks. We wondered what it was. Chief Scout Frank Gruard, who was married to a Cheyenne woman, said it was a graveyard for dead Cheyennes. He said that instead of burying or burning the dead, the Cheyennes laid the body on the roof of the structure and covered it with all the dead person's belongings. The Cheyennes then waited several years until all the flesh was gone before gathering and burying the bones.

One soldier, thinking he might find valuable things up there, climbed to the top of the shade. He found the bones of the dead Indian. He also found a very large, fine blanket and other stuff that he took back to camp. When Lieutenant Bishop found out about the loot, he ordered the soldier to carry it all back and to fix up the burial place as good as before.

General Crook's command camped nearly five days on the Little Missouri River, a muddy stream bordered by many large trees. I had heard so much about the river. I expected to see a wide, deep, foaming and flowing stream. In some places, it flows for three or four miles, dries to sand for a few miles and then rises to running water—just like the Agua Fria in Arizona. Later I learned that the wide Missouri was a river that this stream flowed into.

When we reached the Heart River, everyone felt beaten, and we had not even had a fight. General Crook was more disappointed than anyone. The Sioux had disappeared. We had trailed them for nearly a month in every direction, and we were no closer to them than when we had started out at Goose Creek. Our horses became more starved and exhausted every day we marched, and their riders were in almost as bad a shape. General Crook stopped chasing Sitting Bull at the head of the Heart River.

Ragged and almost starving and freezing to death, we were nearly out of everything except ammunition. The commanders told their men that they must cut down their rations to one hard tack a day. We had no more bacon or coffee and only a little sugar. Many troopers—and I agreed with them—thought we should go to the closest place where we could find food and shelter. We could easily have made it to Fort Abraham Lincoln in four days. While his men went to bed hungry and tried to sleep in cold, damp blankets, General Crook stayed up all night. He had to decide where to go from there. He knew that Deadwood lay due south, but the country in between him and the Black Hills was unexplored. He could go north to Fort Abraham Lincoln, but he believed that the hostiles were hiding out somewhere in the large unknown stretch of country to the south. Crook did not want to leave the Black Hills settlements defenseless. He sent scouts to Fort Laramie with messages to Sheridan to send supplies, and we headed toward the Black Hills.

Some soldiers grumbled quietly among themselves when they heard the general's decision; but the officers, always loyal to their leader, seemed to get new life. Lieutenant Bishop, who was as tired and cold and hungry as I was, said to me with a smile, "We may have a chance to fight the Sioux yet."

22
Horses and Horse Meat
September 6 – 11, 1876

On September 6, we turned south from the Heart River and began a two hundred mile march to the Black Hills. I was lucky to still have my horse. Many cavalrymen plodded along with the infantry because their horses had given out. We camped the first night near the north fork of the Grand River. Nothing grew there, not even sage brush, and we had to gather buffalo chips or manure for the fire. I ate hardtack for supper, and in the morning I drank water with a little sugar. There was no coffee. So General Crook told Lieutenant Bubb, the quartermaster, to take the pack mules to Deadwood, to buy up all the supplies he could and to hurry back. He also sent Major Anson Mills, one hundred fifty Third Cavalrymen, all the best horses and Frank Gruard as guide to find the Black Hills.

The main command moved slowly over the rolling plains because so many soldiers were on foot. Many buffalo roamed about safely because we were not allowed to shoot anything. We made about twelve miles that day. When we finally stopped for the night, we found no water, only a mud hole surrounded by all kinds of animal skeletons.

The next day, we moved on about eighteen miles with no food. Before we reached camp, the men ahead of us had skinned some horses and had given them out to the commanders. We who were behind got nothing from the horses that were killed. Luckily, I noticed one horse with all the flesh gone lying on the ground. Only the whole end of the tail was left. I found plenty of water in a little running stream and boiled the tail into a kind of soup.

When night came on, I overheard several men talk about going somewhere. I was curious and asked where they were going. They said that three miles back on the trail, a horse was lying with its throat cut open. The horse was fat and in good condition, and they were going for the meat. They were taking along their guns and pistols because most likely Indian scouting parties were out there. The Sioux and Cheyenne scouts were always on the lookout for soldiers—especially soldiers straying from the main command. When I lived like an Indian, I had often eaten horses that our warriors had run off from the Pima villages. But for nearly four years, I had lived with the cavalry and had learned that horses were for riding. I was getting pretty hungry for horse meat again.

I told my old friend Lieutenant Bishop, "I'm going with the gang to where a dead horse was."

Bishop replied, "You had better not forget your old Henry rifle."

"That rifle is too heavy for me to carry so far and come back again with some horse meat."

"Well then, take my pistol lying over there. Have something with you so you can fight like a little man."

I thanked Lieutenant Bishop, took his pistol and the belt, and hurried off to catch up with the gang. It was dark, but I ran off in the direction from which we came and caught up with the fifteen soldiers at the crest of the hill.

Sergeant Patrick Lynch, who headed the gang, was an old soldier used to scouting in Indian country. Lynch advised us to move as cautiously and noiselessly as possible, to creep along, never to stand up straight, and to always watch ahead and on both sides of the trail. We crawled as fast as we could, always watching and listening for the sound of horses' hooves. It was a dark, moonless night, but we could see over the edges of the hills toward the west. When we reached the dead horse, the men had a short discussion of how to dispose of it. Some wanted to skin the animal and divide the whole hide; but Sergeant Lynch said not to be so careful about the hide, to take off only the best flesh parts and to be quick about it too. I got the liver and the tongue; the others got the meat.

We hurried out of there following our tracks backward until Lynch told us to halt. He had seen someone moving above us on the edge of the hill. We got down on our knees and crawled all the way to the camp, so we could see any Indians first. We all arrived safely at the camp and in the morning cooked the horse meat for breakfast. When news of the Indians got to the command headquarters, orders were given to watch out for an attack, but there was none. Afterwards, we decided that soon after we had left the skeleton of the dead horse, the Indians had arrived there. It was luck that got us there first and away quickly. If the Indians had arrived before us, they would have gotten all the meat and most likely our hides too. Sergeant Lynch's sensible advice is what saved us.

The next morning after we had marched about five or six miles, a runner came along saying that several hundred Indians had surrounded Major Anson Mills at Slim Buttes about twenty miles away. Major Mills needed help.

Mills' advance party had come upon American Horse's camp near Slim Buttes. After Lieutenant Swatka had driven most of the Indian ponies out of the village, the cavalrymen attacked the camp from two sides and seized its thirty-five tepees. The Indians, driven out of their tepees, took refuge among the rocks on the other side of the river and in a ra-

vine near the camp. Mills feared that Sioux scouts had hurried to the nearby camp of Chief Crazy Horse for rein-
forcements. Mills sent for help.

General Crook ordered all the cavalry to the battle
scene. The cavalrymen with good horses rushed on ahead
not worrying about the soldiers with tired out horses or
without any horses at all who straggled behind in the mud
and rain. Soon the horse I rode got tired, and I could not
keep up with Lieutenant Bishop and the others in Company
G. Soldiers on foot passed me by saying, "You had better
kill that old horse and get a chunk of meat and go on ahead.
You can get over the country faster than that old horse." I
paid no attention to what the soldiers said about my horse. I
did not want to give him up. He was carrying all the things I
had. So I got off my tired horse and led him up the hill. I
traveled alone for some distance. Just as I noticed smoke
coming up between two bluffs, several infantrymen joined
me, and we headed toward American Horse's village. About
two or three miles from the camp, we heard gun reports,
and I hurried on as fast as I could with the old horse.

Just before we reached the village, five cavalry men met
us, pointed to the little hill where we could see all the
smoke. They warned us not to go there because several Indians on the other side of that hill had shot down many soldiers. They also told me that Company G was camped just a
little above the village on Milk Water Creek.

I finally reached Lieutenant Bishop's camp about two
in the afternoon and found him eating something that
smelled very good to a hungry eleven-year-old boy. He told
me to quickly unsaddle my horse and put him with the rest
of the herd. I unloosed the horse as fast as I could and left
him with the soldiers guarding the herd. When I returned to
his camp, Bishop told me to eat some soup of dried buffalo
meat, taken from the Indian village, boiled with wild onions.
He said that while soldiers were fighting it out with the

Cheyennes, others were busy going through the abandoned tepees of the village looking for loot and something to eat. In every tepee the soldiers found many trophies from the Battle of the Little Big Horn and twelve to fifteen rawhide bags filled with dried buffalo meat and gooseberries. The Indian rations became supper for the whole command.

Bishop had already eaten so he and his gun went off to join his men who were all on foot. I was so eager to join the battle that I gulped down the stew and hurried off to find the men in Company G who were going down the left side of the hill to reach the other side of the gulch where most of the fighting was going on. I followed the company down the creek until I met Frank Gruard with fifteen soldiers and three scouts. Gruard, Crook's best scout, was a half breed—part white and part something else besides Indian. He had married a Cheyenne woman, had lived with her tribe for many years, and could speak both the Cheyenne and Sioux languages perfectly. He looked like an Indian and could pass for one. Gruard decided to go over to the mesa behind the gulch. So being a scout myself, I went with him.

After going some distance, we came across the body of a soldier who had died at the beginning of the fight. Other soldiers motioned us to turn back. Just below us, they warned, three or four Indians were crouching in a deep gulch about a hundred yards away and shooting at every soldier who came into their view.

Frank Gruard led the way until we were about twenty-five yards away from the Indians. Gruard told us to remain where we were while he decided what to do. The Indians could not see us as we were behind them and looking across the gulch.

While we waited for Gruard to make up his mind, that daring young man called Buffalo Chips, who had been a partner of Buffalo Bill, reached that gang of soldiers who had warned us to turn back. They were lying on the ground, holding up their guns and shooting into the air. Buffalo Chips said, "What are you shooting at? Why do you not get up on your feet and see what you are shooting at?" Then he said, "Show me where the Indians are, and I will show you how to shoot Indians." The soldiers told Buffalo Chips to crouch down, but he paid them no attention.

We saw Buffalo Chips jump up and run out right in sight of the Indians. Within a few seconds we heard a shot. Buffalo Chips went only about twenty-five yards before he was shot down. The bullet struck first his knee and then went through to his back bone. Buffalo Chips dropped his gun and went head down over the cliff into the creek below. When he hit the water, we saw blood running from his body.

The soldiers just continued to lie on the ground, holding their guns over their heads and shooting in the direction of the Indians. They did this for almost half a day.

Frank Gruard crawled up closer to the place where he thought one Indian was hiding. He kept crawling until the Indian fired another shot. At that moment, with his pistol in his hand, Gruard sprang right up to the smoking gun. He shot twice before the Indian could load his weapon. Three Indians had been hiding out in this gulch. Two had been killed by soldiers firing across the valley. This lone Indian had made a great stand against the soldiers. He probably would have killed more soldiers if not for Frank Gruard's daring deed.

Bugle sounds told me it was time to quit fighting. I had not shot at anything. I went along with some soldiers back toward camp. The cook had boiled more dried buffalo meat for our supper. There was no coffee, no sugar, and no flour to make bread.

After supper General Crook sent Frank Gruard to talk to some Cheyennes who were still hiding in a gulch. Gruard, who could speak their language, told the Indians to come forward if they wanted to live. If they came right out, Gruard said, they would not be harmed, but if they insisted on staying in the gulch, General Crook would order the soldiers to kill them all.

When Frank Gruard had finished talking, a tall man— I think he was Chief Rain in the Face, a northern Cheyenne from the Red Cloud Agency—crawled out of the gulch. He had been shot through the stomach. Other Indians followed. Once about twenty persons had been in that ravine. The sixteen who came out alive were escorted to a tepee where they were guarded by soldiers from the infantry regiment. The chief was taken to a tepee that had been made into a hospital for the wounded soldiers. Three surgeons tried to save him, but he died during the night.

Although General Crook ordered a double guard for the animals, about midnight we heard shots from the banks on the opposite side of the river. The guards then saw Indians driving our horses over the bluffs to the hills. Mounted soldiers went out to gather in the horses and found many animals missing. When General Crook heard this, he said it could not be helped because there were not enough able horses in the whole command to follow the Indians past the mountains. It was just my luck that the horse I had left to be guarded was missing.

I began to worry about the rest of the trip to Deadwood. The companies were getting ready to march again. I was a cavalry scout and I had no horse to ride. Lieutenant Bishop told me to go out and get a pony as there were plenty running around. Two ponies, he said, would be better than one. I took a long rope and ran off to where many ponies were corralled. When I saw one that suited me, I ran up to it and with luck got the rope around its neck. The soldier herding the ponies said to me, "Good for you, boy. Now you have one to ride anyway." I heard the bugles and dared not take time to catch another pony. I led the captured pony to the place where I had left my old horse and found the saddle. Lieutenant Bishop and G Troop had left, and General Crook's headquarters was moving out with the sixteen prisoners.

I quickly saddled up and put my camping outfit on my pony. Then I got on that new pony of mine and went by the burning villages and the burning bodies of the Cheyenne. Going down the creek, I passed the place where Buffalo Chips got his last medicine. As I whipped my pony on, I heard soldiers yelling at me to go faster because the Cheyennes were on my heels.

I took no time heading for the hills. As I went on, I could hear shots behind me. One bullet struck some stones that glanced up to my legs. I dropped from the pony. I thought the bullet had struck me. I got up and touched my leg. I felt no blood. Looking to the left down the valley, I noticed several Indians bolt across the creek. Others above the creek moved across the valley to head me off at the top of the hill. Eight or ten Indians were only two hundred yards behind me. I began to think that this was the last day for me to see this world. Then I said to myself, "I will shoot every Indian I see until my cartridges are gone." Soon I became very weak and expected every moment to be shot by those behind.

I dared not look back any more; then suddenly I heard bullets coming from the direction in which I was headed whistling over my head. I glanced up the hill ahead of me. To my great surprise and relief, I saw rows of cavalrymen shooting. Finally, someone yelled down to me to come on up. It was my fatherly friend, Bishop. He came down to meet me. "Mike, I'm happy to see you alive," he said. "I feared I would see you with your head off."

I thought that a god had sent Lieutenant Bishop to rescue me. Bishop had brought back his whole company for the sake of finding me dead on the battlefield. If Bishop had the same kind of heart like other white men, I would have been tortured alive. If the Cheyennes had reached me and discovered that I was another kind of Indian, they would have treated me worse than any white person. Bishop had such a kind, loving feeling about me that he could not bear to think how the Indians would treat me.

Lieutenant Bishop led me over to the hill where a soldier was holding my pony. When I was thoroughly rested, I ate some dried meat, got on my pony, and we followed the soldiers. Lieutenant Bishop asked me how I got left behind and nearly killed. I told him the best I could, and we laughed the whole time.

That night I joined some men gathering wood. There was not much wood, and I returned to camp with only a little. I looked over to where I had tied my pony. He was gone. General Crook had ordered that all ponies captured at Slim Buttes be turned over to the quartermaster and slaughtered for rations. While Lieutenant Bishop was visiting another officer, soldiers from General Crook's headquarters came and took my pony away. I asked Lieutenant Bishop to write a note to General Crook explaining how I had almost sacrificed my life to get that pony. He wrote the note and told me to be quick about taking it to the general.

When I arrived at General Crook's camp, he was glad to see me. He took hold of my hands with both of his hands and asked how he could help me. After he read the note he said, "My Apache boy, I am very sorry we took your only pony away from you. I will do everything possible to get it back to you, but it may be too late now."

Crook quickly wrote a note to take to the quartermaster, and he told me to hurry. When I arrived at the quartermaster all out of breath, Lieutenant Bubb read the note and told me to look at the ponies that were left. I looked and looked but could not find my pony in the bunch. The officer told me that he must have been one of the first killed. He could not help me now. I was in despair and almost cried when I heard that my pony had been killed.

The next morning, there was only pony meat for breakfast. Lieutenant Bishop said that pony meat tasted much better than horse meat. Hungry as I was, I could hardly swallow the meat thinking it might be the pony I had risked my life for and had lost. Lieutenant Bishop told me I had to join the foot gang for the rest of the campaign and to take a chunk of cooked pony meat for lunch.

23
The Foot Brigade
September 11 — October 24, 1876

Early the next morning, I joined the foot brigade—a long line of about eight hundred men. Some horses had given out, others had been stolen by the Cheyennes, and the rest had been eaten for dinner. A few officers were there too. Twenty-five men were badly injured and unable to ride a horse or walk. Each injured man was placed on a litter that was attached to the packsaddle of a mule, and he rode behind it.

Before the sun was up, we began our long march. I carried my blanket and a tiny bundle of pony meat on my back—all that I had to keep me alive. The foot brigade trekked down a steep rocky slope for a few miles and came to the barren Bad Lands where no grass or bushes grew in the clay-covered valleys or on the hills. Occasionally, we saw some prickly pear cacti, but the fruit was all gone.

All day we marched in the hot sun through this empty desert land. Late in the afternoon when the soldiers on horseback had made camp and we on foot were still plodding on, a light rain fell upon us. Soon several soldiers came riding toward us. They came back to let their comrades ride the last few miles into camp. Nobody met me with a horse to ride. When I reached Lieutenant Bishop's camp, he shared some cooked pony meat with me. The next morning I had a few bites of pony meat and was back marching with the foot brigade.

On the third day after the Battle of Slim Buttes, we began our final terrible forty-mile march through the Bad Lands at daybreak. Rain had fallen all night, and the ground was soaked. We walked through mud so thick and sticky that whenever I lifted my foot, it brought up about ten pounds of clay. By late afternoon I was so weak with hunger, I thought I could walk no longer. I had eaten my last piece of pony meat the day before and had nothing more.

When I saw several men straying off the trail, I became curious and staggered after them. They always made for the gopher holes around which wild onions grew. As soon as we picked the little plants we plopped them right into our mouths. When we came upon many prickly pear cacti, the boys burned off the thorns and then cut them in chunks to eat. The prickly pear meat did not taste so good, but I ate some just to have something in my stomach and stay alive.

We marched far into the night. It was so dark that we could not stay on the trail. The command became scattered, and some of the wounded were thrown from the mule litters by the stumbling and jumping animals. Once in awhile, the boys up ahead whistled for us to follow. Many men were sick from hunger and almost crazy. I heard much sniffling and even grown-up men sobbing in their misery. I did not cry, but I felt like it.

We finally reached the Belle Fourche of the Cheyenne River. Lieutenant Bishop gave me some dried gooseberries for my supper. The pony meat was all gone. As we set up camp in a nice green meadow where wild fruit trees grew, I heard—I was always listening in those days—that several boys who were tired of the soldier's life strayed from the command and killed themselves. Someone else said that Indians had scalped two men in sight of a whole company. We had no able horses or men to go after the murderers.

The next morning—four days after the Battle of Slim Buttes—the sun shone brightly for the first time in nearly two weeks. We did not move camp that day. Several men wandered off; some went up the creek; others went down it; I went off too. The creek bottom was full of wild plum trees. Some men shook the trees until the fruit fell to the ground. I picked some up and ate until I was sick.

After we had eaten too many plums, we felt very tired. So we sat upon the ground and talked all kinds of foolishness to cheer each other. I asked if anyone knew what country we were in and in what direction we were going. One soldier with his senses left in him said that we were at the north end of the Black Hills.

As the soldier pointed toward the Black Hills, we saw something moving. Another soldier said that soon many wagons with rations for the entire command would come from Deadwood. That soldier knew what he was talking about. Cowboys driving one hundred seventy-five cattle and one hundred fifty wagons filled with good stuff to eat were heading our way. We all cheered when the herd of beef cattle came into view. The wagons came soon after, and people from the towns came to welcome the soldiers who had come through so much hardship and danger to save them from massacre.

Nearly all day long we watched the wagons with flour and vegetables coming. When the wagons passed us, we followed them into camp. Toward evening soldiers from every company went to the quartermaster for double rations. They returned with loads of good food on their backs. That night we ate all we wanted. The steaming cups of coffee and the bacon and the flapjacks tasted so good. The command was ordered to remain in camp the next day, eat all we could and clean our guns. That night before I fell asleep under cover of a canvas tent with a clean dry blanket, I thought my troubles were over, and I think everybody else felt the same.

During the night, I woke up with stomach pains and diarrhea. Oh! I thought I was going to die. Every time I lay down I had to get up again. The whole camp suffered. Doctor Clements announced that the diarrhea was caused from eating too much on an empty stomach. Three doctors were on their feet the whole day going to every camp giving medicine to the men. The next day we were well again and could eat good square meals.

General Crook wanted to continue the Yellowstone Expedition using the Black Hills as his base. But General Sheridan, Crook's boss, decided to disband the expedition and organize a new one. Crook was called to the agency at Fort Robinson to help round up all the Indians there. On September 16, 1876, General Crook and a small escort left us for Fort Laramie. General Wesley Merritt was now in charge. Major John Upham commanded Company G, and Lieutenant Hall Bishop was second in command.

On September 18, we moved on toward the Black Hills. No one brought us horses, so I stayed in the foot brigade. We camped in a meadow surrounded by wooded hills near a little town called Crook City. General Merritt intended to stay there two to three days, but the men could not be good. The first night many soldiers got drunk and started fighting. So Merritt ordered a march on toward Deadwood.

Because all the soldiers and the horses that still lived were all worn out, we traveled only a short distance the next day. We camped about fifteen miles from Deadwood on a little stream called Box Elder for the trees that grew along its banks. General Merritt sent in only a few men with pack trains and wagons for provisions. While we camped there, along came a caravan of artillery men who shared their oats and corn with the Fifth Cavalry horses.

We headed toward Rapid City marching through the thick pines and passing many prosperous mining towns. When we arrived at Custer City, we found all the stores and houses deserted. Although the men had nearly revived in the cool clear air with plenty to eat, the horses could go no farther. We camped several weeks along French Creek, moving only when the grass was gone. The mornings and evenings were getting rather cool, so we sat around the camp fire most of the time. The men told stories and sang songs. When the mail arrived, the men would read their letters. Some read them aloud. Almost everybody but me got letters. I had no family to write to me, and I still could not read.

One fine sunny day, I saw men and even officers taking off their clothes and shaking them over the fire laughing. I heard one officer say, "This will kill the bugs that have been biting me all night and keeping me from sleep." I had thought I was the only one who was lousy. We had no change of clothing for two months. In the early part of August, we left our extra clothing behind at Goose Creek; now it was late October.

On October 22, the Fifth Cavalry camped outside the Red Cloud Agency where we had camped in July after chasing the Cheyennes all the way from War Bonnet Creek. Lieutenant Bishop thought we were there to take part in ending the campaign by disarming all the reservation Indians, but the Fifth took no part in rounding up the Indians. All the warriors who remained on the Red Cloud Reservation surrendered quietly and meekly to General Mackenzie and the Fourth Cavalry at Fort Robinson. Most of the Sioux had scattered all over the Northwest while Chief Sitting Bull had headed for Canada.

I did not attend the closing ceremonies. Bishop told me that General Crook was there and had praised all the troops for their effort and sacrifice in the Big Horn-Yellowstone Campaign.

On October 24, General Sheridan ordered General Merritt and five companies of the Fifth Cavalry to proceed from Fort Robinson to Fort Brown about two hundred miles away. As I had no horse—the pony I wanted for my own was killed and eaten on the way to the Black Hills—I rode in a wagon for six days. At least I did not have to walk. I was no longer in the foot brigade.

General Merrit and the Officers of the Fifth Cavalry 1876
Drawing from Charles King's *Campaigning with Crook*

24

Shoshones, Cheyennes, Arapahos and Bannocks
November 1876 — June 1879

I was glad we did not stay long at Fort Sidney. The surrounding country was so barren—no shrubs or trees grew there—and the nights were very cold. One night, several men from M Troop got drunk. Two troopers got very drunk and lay down on the freezing ground. Next morning they were found frozen to death.

From Fort Sidney we followed the Platte River for three days to Fort McPherson. We passed a town called North Platte, but we did not stop there for fear more soldiers would get drunk with the same results as at Fort Sidney. Three companies took their station here, but Companies G and M were ordered to Fort Brown in Wyoming Territory, near the Shoshone Indian Reservation.

The Shoshone Reservation was located on the Wind River and was the best I have ever seen. Chief Washakie, an important friend of the United States, got everything for his people that a reservation should have. The government gave Chief Washakie a school, a church, a mill, a hospital, farm implements and seed, and an army post to help protect the Shoshones from their enemies.

Many who saw Chief Washakie said he looked just like George Washington. I believed them, but I had never seen Washington, and at that time I had not even seen his picture. The chief was big and tall, a fine looking man, with long white hair thrown back over his forehead. When he came to the post to visit the commanding officer, he always rode a white horse and his three sons followed him. The oldest was a big fat man; the others were just middle-sized young men. A medicine man wearing a great war bonnet with many feathers went everywhere with Washakie. I often watched this medicine man start to smoke the peace pipe when the Indians and the officers sat around in a circle on the ground. He always did the same thing. He first held the pipe high in the air and then brought it down to the ground before he placed it in his mouth to smoke. He passed it to another Indian who did the same as the medicine man. The pipe was passed around the circle until all had smoked. The chief always got the pipe last.

Fort Brown was situated about three miles from the Shoshone Indian Agency. This country was over a mile high, just east of the Continental Divide and just south of the Grand Tetons. Not far to the south was the famous South Pass where, Lieutenant Bishop said, many years earlier the forty-niners bound for California and Oregon-bound pioneers passed. I think Fort Brown is the highest United States military post. Many streams flow from the mountains into the White River so game and fish were plentiful.

The wood for buildings on the post came from trees growing high up in the mountains. No wagon road went up that far. Wood cutters threw the logs into the creek, and the swift waters carried them down to the post where they were stopped by a dam. This was the way the quartermaster brought wood to the post.

Two creeks came together near Fort Brown. Soldiers often went out fishing and returned with a mess of trout. Sometimes twelve to fifteen officers and men went farther north to Bull Lake, a lake in a deep rocky canyon about one and a half miles wide and seven miles long. They always returned to the post with many fish of all sizes, some weighing fifteen pounds. They were wonderful fish with hardly any bones, and they did not have a bad taste like some muddy water fish.

About three miles from the post, yellowish water seeped out of the hillside and settled on the flat surface below as a thick mass of tar. This place was called Tar Lake. Soldiers from Fort Brown went out in wagons to gather the tar that was mixed with gravel to make very good roofs and sidewalks.

Even closer to the post was another important small lake about one hundred fifty yards long and sixty yards wide. Right at the center of the lake, hot water bubbled up. People with rheumatism and other diseases believed that if they bathed in the Hot Spring, they would be cured. In those days I was young, spry and a good foot racer, and I had never had a serious illness. The water tasted sulfurous. Some people drank the smelly and bad tasting water for their health. I never drank any, but I liked to bathe in the nice warm water.

Because of that Hot Spring, I think I ruined my health. One day, I borrowed a horse to ride down to the valley. As I rode up to that Hot Spring, it looked too good to pass by without first taking a wash. I quickly tied the horse to a bush, removed my clothes and jumped into the lake. The warm water came up to my neck and felt so good. I enjoyed myself until I heard a horse running. I turned my head and looked at the bush where I had tied my horse; he was not there. Half dressed and shoes in my hands, I ran down the road toward the post, scared that the horse might stray to

another road and go to another country and that someone
might catch him on the way home. I had borrowed a new
saddle, a bridle and a good horse too. I ran as fast as I
could. It began to snow, and the wind blew hard in my face.
Half out of breath, I walked a little way; then I ran again. I
reached the corral at last. The horse had returned. I had no
need to run after him all that distance like a fool.

I became a very sick boy with pain all over my body
and coughing all the time. The doctor said I had pneumonia
and that I could not live long, but Lieutenant Bishop doc-
tored me with some brandy mixed with hot water. In a few
days, I could eat and drink anything, and within two weeks I
was on my feet.

Before that happened to me, I could beat anybody in a
foot race at any distance—seventy-five yards, two hundred
yards or three miles. I used to be able to keep up with
horses running five to seven miles. I got much practice
when I was in the foot brigade.

There was an old prospector from Montana who
wanted to run a foot race with somebody. The boys in
Company G got up a purse of one hundred fifty dollars for
me to race this man. I easily beat him at fifteen yards. Then
he wanted to run two hundred yards for double the money. I
politely declined to run that distance. I thought it was too
far for me to make good time. But the boys said, "Oh hell,
run anyway; you can beat the old man at any distance." As I
ran, I stepped on a little stone and tripped and fell. I got up
to run again, but I could not catch up with the old man. He
passed the finish line only five feet ahead of me. After that, I
never did any foot racing.

In the spring of 1878, about seven hundred fifty Northern Cheyennes and Arapahos—I think from Fort Sheridan,
Nebraska—made their homes about three miles down the

creek from the post near Tar Lake. Chief Washakie said
they could stay if they did no mischief. I used to visit the
young Arapaho lads and sometimes would stay down there
for two or three days. In a few months, I could understand
the Arapaho language and could use their sign language.
Most all the Plains Indians used signs. When they met one
another, they always used their hands. I never knew any
Southwest Indians who used signs. It was good to know the
hand sign language. Then you could do business whenever
you met a Plains Indian.

Early in September 1878, news came from headquarters in Omaha that a band of Bannock Indians from Fort
Hall, Idaho was on the warpath and heading toward Yellowstone National Park. Nobody knew that the Shoshones
were related to these Bannock Indians. Lieutenant Bishop
with fifty of his best men from Company G, seventy-five
scouts from the Northern Cheyennes and Arapahos and
fifty Shoshones set out to cut off the Bannocks. I went with
my old friend. In whatever peril he undertook, I was always
with him. I was then two years older than I had been during
the Sioux War, and I was ready to be in any kind of fight or
trouble.

We followed the Wind River for two days until we
came to its head about fifteen miles from Yellowstone Park.
The stream was so narrow that I could jump across it in
many places. Lieutenant Bishop ordered twenty-five troopers and twenty-five Indian scouts to search through the
country for the Bannock Indians. If they should find the
Bannocks and they refused to surrender, he said to shoot
them. The Cheyennes and Arapahos agreed, but the
Shoshones did not care to go.

They started out early in the morning. The Indian
scouts went out ahead of the cavalrymen. In the afternoon
the Indian scouts returned. Arrayed in great war style, they
dashed back and forth through the camp beating on their

drums made from head skins, singing war songs and hoisting poles to which scalps were tied.

Later the detachment of troopers returned with eighteen captured women and children. The sergeant reported that the Indian scouts had killed seven men. He did not know the number of Bannocks who had escaped because he was not there during the killing. He said that the Cheyenne and Arapaho scouts would have killed more Bannocks, but the Shoshones came just in time to save some of them.

That night the Cheyennes and Arapahos were preparing to have a great victory celebration. Chief Washakie of the Shoshones went to Lieutenant Bishop and asked him to stop the singing and dancing. He said that the dead Bannocks were part of the Shoshone people. When Chief Washakie was a young man in his twenties, he had lived with the Bannocks. Washakie said if the Cheyennes and Arapahos did not stop this kind of singing and dancing, the Shoshones would have to fight them.

Lieutenant Bishop ordered the Cheyennes and Arapahos not to have a victory dance. He said they could have a social dance, but not to bring out any scalps. There was no dance of any kind.

Afterwards through interpreters, we learned from a captured woman that only two small parties of Bannocks had left the reservation, and the other party was heading back to it. They had come in this direction to visit their Shoshone relatives. She said that the seven persons who escaped into the hills might have gone to the Shoshone Agency.

The next morning Lieutenant Bishop decided it was about time to head home. Rations were getting short and there were prisoners to feed too. Lieutenant Bishop sent out a hunting party to kill something to eat. He said that if they happened to see any kind of cattle, it would be all right to kill one or two. About eight men soon returned with two live steers that they killed right in the camp. That night we had much to eat, and the next day we broke camp and began our three day return march to Fort Brown.

When we returned to the post, we turned the prisoners over to Chief Washakie. Bishop warned the Cheyennes and the Arapahos not to celebrate. If they celebrated, he said, the Shoshones might jump the whole camp. The Bannock Indians had not killed anybody or stolen any Indians, so you could say they were not bad Indians. They were only away from the Fort Hall Reservation. Word came that one Bannock party had returned to their reservation. The Bannocks who came with us to the Shoshone Reservation were ordered to return to their homes. That was the end of the scare that started the Bannock War. This was the last time I went out on an Indian campaign with Lieutenant Bishop.

I learned later that the Indian agent at Fort Hall wanted some Bannock families to move to another place that they did not like. The Indians were happy where they were. When the agent threatened to have soldiers make them move, many Bannocks went back to the hills where they used to live. They did not hurt or kill anyone and did not steal anything belonging to another people. The Indians told their story before an investigating committee. The agent was fired.

Second Lieutenant Bishop was promoted to first lieutenant in June 1879 and was ordered to join Company A of the Fifth Cavalry commanded by Captain Jacob Auger at Fort Russell. In September Bishop and I said good-bye to all our friends in Company G, the company I had lived with since my capture seven years earlier. We boarded a stage going to Greene River and from there we took a train to Cheyenne and Fort Russell.

25

Forts Russell and Laramie
September 1879 — September 1881

About a month after Lieutenant Bishop joined his new company, all six companies at Fort Russell were ordered to move out toward the Ute Reservation on the White River, one hundred seventy miles away, to rescue Major Thomas Thornburg's command.

Before 1850 the Utes, who roamed the mountains and deserts of Colorado, Utah, southern Wyoming and northern New Mexico, never saw many white men. After gold was discovered in Colorado, the whites forced the Utes to sign away most of their land. Now white men were trying to drive them from their reservation on the White River.

Chief Ouray, a wise leader who spoke English, Spanish and several Indian languages, was once a friend of Kit Carson. He worked hard to protect the rights of his people and to keep the peace. Agent Meeker tried to force the Utes to accept Christianity and to plow the land on which the Utes' horses grazed. The Utes wanted to keep their old ways. In September 1879, a Ute medicine man named Canello was so angry that he hit Meeker and knocked him down.

One hundred fifty troops under Major Thornburgh came to the reservation to straighten things out. Before the soldiers and the Indians could get together for a talk,

Thornburgh was shot dead, and the Utes surrounded and attacked the army wagons. The troops needed help.

The command from Fort Russell was gone for two months. Lieutenant Bishop did not want me to go with him this time. He had a house, much furniture and a new buggy that he wanted me to look after. I did not mind staying behind in a warm house and in a place where there was enough to eat. I did not care much about going anywhere when it was freezing. Before Lieutenant Bishop left, he arranged for me to board at cost with a detachment that was left behind, agreeing to make it right when he returned. He also allowed me to get necessary things at the sutler's store, not to exceed twelve dollars a month.

By the time the Fifth Cavalry reached Milk River, the Utes had been shooting at the army wagons for almost a week. Thirteen soldiers had died and forty-eight were wounded. The Fifth soon drove the Indians off, and Chief Ouray surrendered. At the reservation, the soldiers discovered that Indians had killed Meeker and nine other civilians and had taken Meeker's wife and daughter, another woman and two children as hostages.

Government representatives came from Washington D.C. to meet with Chief Ouray. The chief agreed to release the captives in exchange for his people's freedom. The Utes went back to their homes on the White River. The next year, after Bishop and I had left that place, Ouray died and the Utes were forced to leave their reservation.

In the spring of 1880, the entire Fifth Cavalry under General Wesley Merritt moved from Fort Russell to Fort Laramie. Lieutenant Bishop knew how I was eager I was to become a civilized Indian. I was then nearly fifteen years old. I had done much traveling and been in many Indian battles, but I could neither read nor write. Lieutenant Bishop got permission for me to go to the post day school with the children of the officers and soldiers. Each night, I brought home all my books. Lieutenant Bishop, seeing how eager I was to learn, often helped me to get my lessons ready for the next day. In only four months, I went ahead of all the little children in my class and got to second grade. The next year I studied in a class all by myself. During the summer of 1881, I did not go to school. A discharged soldier from Company B, Fifth Cavalry, whom I knew well, was the contractor for the United States Post Office at Fort Laramie. He asked me to ride the mail route to Fort Sidney about one hundred miles away. The contractor said I could have four horses to change about every twenty-five miles. Other men usually made it in three days for fifteen dollars. He said that if I made the trip in two days, I would get my money quicker. So I told the man I would take the job.

I started off early one morning and got to Fort Sidney before sundown. After two bottles of beer and a pretty good dinner, I mounted a fresh horse and started out in the dark. After I left the last station, I could not see the trail and strayed off the road. I unsaddled my horse, tied him to a tree, and using a large overcoat for a cover soon fell asleep. I learned by this experience that sometimes it is smart not to hurry. The next trip I made in three days.

I made only three trips carrying mail for the government. The night after my last trip to Sidney Bridge, Lieutenant Bishop told me that General Wesley Merritt, the Fifth Cavalry commander, wanted to see me in his quarters. I had been with General Merritt since the Campaign of 1876, and we often had a little talk when he saw Lieutenant Bishop and me together. He thought a lot of Lieutenant Bishop who was a fine young man and a very good officer.

Lieutenant Bishop went with me to General Merritt's quarters. The general gave me much advice about my future. He had heard about my quick progress in school, how in just a few months I had learned to read and all there was to learn in the post school. "No man," he said, "can succeed unless he has a good education. You must learn about other men and follow their examples. You are young and strong, ready to take on anything. If you stay around soldiers all the time, you will never learn much or get ahead. Most young soldiers cannot read or write their own names. All they care about is getting something to eat and something to wear without paying for it. After they get out of the army, they cannot make a respectable living. When you get an education you can do more than the common man. You can become a teacher, a lawyer or an officer in the army." General Merritt wanted me to go away to school in the East.

Lieutenant Bishop asked me if I would like to leave the company and go to school in the East to learn something that would make a man of me. Without considering the matter much, I said, "Yes, I will go any place you think will be good for me."

About two months later, General Merritt received a letter from the Secretary of the Interior in Washington D.C. The general showed Lieutenant Bishop the letter and told him to go to the quartermaster and arrange for my long journey.

In September 1881, Lieutenant Hall Bishop accompanied me on the government stage to Cheyenne and saw me off on the east bound Union-Pacific. After we found my seat in the car, we both held our hands together, and we both shed tears. I thought about all the hard times we had together in the past; how when I was sick, he nursed me and loved me as his own child. I respected him as a father. That day when we parted, I feared we would never meet again.

Part IV

Mike's Eastern
Education
1881 — 1885

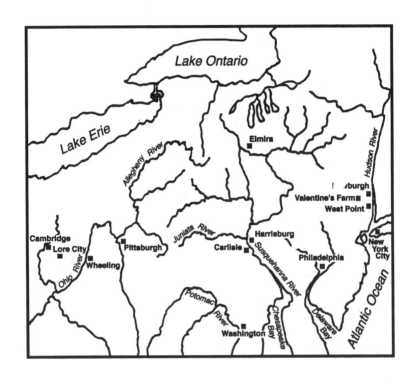

Lake Ontario

Lake Erie

Allegheny River

Elmira

Hudson River

/burgh

Valentine's Farm

West Point

Cambridge

Lore City

Juniata River

Pittsburgh

Ohio River

Wheeling

Carlisle

Harrisburg

Susquehanna River

Philadelphia

New York City

Atlantic Ocean

Potomac River

Chesapeake Bay

Delaware Bay

Washington

An Eastern Education
1881-1887

26
Carlisle Indian School
September 1881 – May 1882

Lieutenant Bishop had telegraphed Captain Earl Thomas, and my old friend met me as I stepped off the train in Omaha. Captain Thomas was at that time the chief quartermaster for the Department of the Platt. We had not seen each other for over five years, so we had much to talk about as we rode in the ambulance to his quarters about four miles away. I was very happy to see Mrs. Thomas, the woman who always looked after me at Date Creek Camp when Major Burns was out in the field. Mrs. Thomas was also very pleased to see me. She looked me all over and said that I had grown up into a handsome young man. She was most pleased that I spoke such good English and that I could read and write, too.

That evening Captain Thomas took me to General George Crook's house. General and Mrs. Crook remembered me well. It was almost exactly four years since I had last seen the general. I had not seen Mrs. Crook since 1875 at Fort Whipple when I had often visited her with Mrs. Burns and her two small children.

They both greeted me warmly and wished me great success in my new undertaking. General Crook said, "This schooling is a great thing. That is how the white men got the best of the Indians. Now, you are an Indian and an Apache, too. The white men think all Apaches are very bad Indians and do not want them to have a chance to be worth anything. But you will do your best to get a thorough education and become useful to your people. Make the white people change their minds. Many think the only good Indians are dead Indians. But the living ones are better yet."

As smart as General Crook was, he always thought all the Indians in Arizona, except perhaps the Pimas, were Apaches. Mrs. Crook thought the same. All the Indians were treated as if they were Apaches. My people were called Apache-Mohaves by most white people, but we are not Apaches. We are Yavapais. After a long, friendly talk, General and Mrs. Crook bid me a happy future. They said I was still young and had plenty of time to improve myself.

I spent the night at the Thomas' quarters. We stayed up some time remembering the old days after I was captured and especially the good times when I stayed with Mrs. Thomas. We also talked about all the people we knew and the things that had happened since we had last been together. The next morning after breakfast, Captain Thomas took me to the depot in Omaha city. Before I got on the train, he gave me a twenty dollar greenback and told me to make it last as long as I could. As the train pulled out, we both shed tears. He was the only one left to see me going off to a new life. He was with Captain Burns when the soldiers picked me up near the Four Peaks in December 1872, and he was the very first officer to call me Mike. James Burns had given me his name, and since then I have always been called Michael, Mickie or Mike Burns.

I then rode east to Chicago, Illinois where I changed to a train going to Harrisburg, Pennsylvania. Captain Thomas had given me a note to show the conductor who told me what to do. At Harrisburg, I telegraphed Captain Pratt to meet me at the Carlisle Indian School. I arrived at the school late in September 1881.

Captain P. H. Pratt was a veteran of the Civil War and the Plains Wars. Later, he escorted Cheyenne and Arapaho prisoners in chains from Fort Sill, Indian Territory to Saint Augustine, Florida and lived with them there. Pratt wanted to improve the Indians' lives by sending them to good schools where they could learn something useful. He even went to Washington and talked to congressmen.

In 1880—one year before my arrival there—Pratt turned the abandoned army barracks at Carlisle, Pennsylvania into a non-reservation school. Carlisle Barracks was built of stone during the Revolutionary War. General George Washington used it as his headquarters, and later prisoners of war lived there. During the Civil War, the Northern Army used the buildings to recruit soldiers. After the war it became a home for old soldiers. Now, Carlisle Barracks had a better use—to educate young Indians to learn the white man's ways so that the Indian race could be saved.

Captain Pratt was the superintendent of the Carlisle Indian School; and Dr. Givens, Miss Robertson and Mr. Campbell were his assistants. The one hundred seventy pupils came from many Indian tribes. I was the only one from the far Southwest—a Yavapai Indian from Arizona. I did not come from a reservation but through the request of General Wesley Merritt, the commanding army officer at Fort Laramie, Wyoming Territory.

In many ways, I was more fortunate than most other students. I had lived with the white men for nearly ten years and was used to their customs. All students were required to speak only English. Since the teachers could not speak the Indian languages, interpreters were needed in the classroom. Captain Pratt gave an order that children speaking their own tongue would be punished. Other Carlisle students, many older and many others younger than I, knew no English at all. Captain Pratt's order did not bother me in the least. I was the only Indian from Arizona and had no companion from my tribe. Anyway, I could no longer speak or understand the language of my people because I was taken away from them when I was only seven or eight years old.

Soon after entering the school, all students were given an English name. My adopted father had named me Mike Burns many years earlier. It was a very upsetting for Indian boys to have their long hair cut. Captain Burns and Lieutenant Thomas had cut my long black hair soon after I made my home with G Company.

Many students were luckier than I. They had fathers— some of them important chiefs—and mothers to return to when their school days were over. Some boys even had brothers and sisters in the school. If their father was an important chief, he sometimes came to visit them.

The boys and girls were together in the classroom. By this time I could speak and understand English very well, and I was beginning to read and write the language. I had already been promoted to third grade at Fort Laramie. There were no others in that grade so I had to study by myself.

Everyone went to school in the morning and worked the other half day. We had all kinds of duties just as soldiers do, and we learned as we worked. I learned carpentry and painting first and then blacksmithing. On other days, I worked in the fields or in the dairy. Congress was slow in sending money to help run the school, so the students worked to eat and to keep the buildings from falling down.

A bugle woke us each morning at six, and taps sent us to bed at night. Sometimes, I played that bugle. While I was a little boy living with the soldiers at Fort Whipple in Arizona in 1873 and 1874, I learned to blow one. At Carlisle I soon became a first-class bugler.

Breakfast was served at seven o'clock in a dining room large enough for all the students to eat at long tables at the same time. At meal time when the bell rang, all the boys came together in lines, just like soldiers. One boy was the first sergeant at the head of the companies. Mr. Campbell, a white man, called the names, and each boy answered promptly. If a boy was late, he was not allowed to eat. If he was absent, he was sent to the guardhouse.

We slept in large dormitories. Each boy had a black enameled bed, a chair and a box that served as a trunk where he could keep his belongings. When the first Indians came to Carlisle, there were no beds, and the boys had to sleep on the hard cold floor. We kept our rooms very clean.

Captain Pratt had strict rules. We had to obey orders just like soldiers. Each day Captain Pratt or one of his staff came to our rooms for inspection. We had to stand very straight while they looked us all over to see that our hair was combed, our clothes brushed and our shoes shined. They checked to see that our beds were made right and looked in our wooden boxes to see that our clothing was clean and repaired. No one was permitted to smoke.

The students wore uniforms to class. They were made by students studying to be tailors. The uniforms were just like cavalry uniforms, blue with narrow stripes of red down the outside seam of the trousers. We could wear our own clothing away from the school.

On Saturdays, the boys policed the whole school grounds. On Sunday mornings, we went to Sunday School, and in the afternoon we heard Dr. Lippincott of Carlisle preach a sermon in the school chapel. He was a good speaker, and when he preached the gospel he touched almost everyone's heart. Since that time I have never heard such good preaching about God's son, Jesus Christ. We could go to any church we wished, and I often went into town to hear others preach, but they did not give me such good feelings. Congress was slow in sending money to the school, and the generous people in local churches helped keep it going.

When I was not going to classes or doing hard labor, I taught the other boys to play baseball. I had learned to play the game when I was with the soldiers at Fort Brown, Fort Russell and Fort Laramie. Once in the spring of 1878, I was a catcher when the soldiers at Fort Brown played against a team of civilians in a town called Landers. Someone had given the Carlisle school many bats and balls, but none of these Indian boys knew a thing about baseball, and they had a hard time learning to play. Some boys practiced throwing and catching balls nearly every day until after a while they were like experienced throwers and catchers. Then they learned to bat balls in the air, and they kept on throwing and catching. In a few months, they divided into teams and played baseball in a square. Later, I measured out a real baseball diamond. At last I had them playing pretty good baseball.

I did not care to play football. It was too dangerous. I saw a boy get killed once when two were running after one ball in the air. As one boy tried to catch the flying football in his hands, the other came up from the opposite direction and kicked at it. He kicked at the same time the other boy was right under him looking at the ball. The boy on the ground was kicked right in the stomach, and he fell back on the ground and never again got up. Watching that kind of ball playing was enough for me.

The boys got to be great baseball players, and they played against many college teams. They also played football, and they took the championship in the United States, I believe in 1906. I did not stay long enough at Carlisle Indian School to play in any of these games.

Things were not always good for many students. Many studied trades they did not like and that were of no use when they left the school. Some became ill and died without their families knowing anything about it. I believe the cause was the change in living and the different food. I was more fortunate, I studied trades that were very useful in later years, and I was never sick while I was at that school.

Captain Pratt asked me if I wanted to spend the summer working on a farm in New York State. I then remembered the talks I had ten years earlier at Date Creek Camp with Mrs. Fanny Corbusier about that place. I was always eager for new adventures, and I thought about it only a few minutes before I said, "Yes."

A Nineteenth Century Farm in New York State
From an old print.

27

Valentine's Farm, West Point and New York City
May 1882 – May 1883

Captain Pratt sent me to a farm close to the Hudson River in Orange County, New York. This place was owned by a Mr. Valentine of New York City who had invented varnishing and owned two or three large stores in New York City. He paid me only eighteen dollars a month. Valentine's farm was located nine miles south of Newburgh and about seven miles west of the Military Academy at West Point. The farm's main crop was apples, but we milked one hundred seventy-five cows every night. Eight other Carlisle boys, including Almarine McKellip, a Creek Indian, worked with me on the farm. Mary, a Pueblo Indian girl from a reservation north of Albuquerque, New Mexico, helped in the house. Each day we hoed corn or picked apples, and at about three o'clock we began to milk the cows. The milk was loaded on the nearby railroad cars to be taken to New York City.

When the harvest season was over, Almarine and Mary and the others went back to the Carlisle school. I accepted the offer to stay and work on the farm evenings and before breakfast for eighteen dollars a month plus room and board.

I had the opportunity to go to a country school two miles away. When I learned that my friend General Wesley Merritt was the superintendent of the United States Military Academy, I wrote him a letter telling him about all I had done since leaving Fort Laramie. He soon wrote to me asking me to visit him at West Point. I took the letter to our foreman Major Alvoh and asked for permission to visit West Point. Alvoh was an old army officer who had known the general in the Civil War, and he needed little time to consider my wishes before he approved them.

I was very excited about visiting West Point, the place where General Crook and most of the officers I knew in the Fifth Cavalry including my best friend Lieutenant Hall Bishop had been educated. I walked swiftly to the railroad station three miles away and got on the train to Newburgh where I ran to catch a boat going down the Hudson River about fifteen miles to West Point.

The captain of the little boat was very friendly. He asked me where I was going. I told him I was going to visit General Merritt who was commanding West Point. The captain asked, "How long have you known the general?"

I said, "I was out on campaigns against the Sioux in 1876 after they killed General Custer and all his men. General Merritt was in charge of all the Fifth Cavalry then. I was also with him at Fort Laramie. He is the one who told me to go to Carlisle School. That is why I am here. I have not seen him since, and I live too close to him not to visit. It would be a shame not to meet an old-time friend when I have the chance to do so."

"Well," the captain said, "I am an old friend of General Merritt, too. Therefore, I will gladly take you on my boat to see him."

When he asked if I had killed any Sioux, I told him that I could not say for sure about killing any. I had shot into a whole lot of them many times, but not at close range. I was quite sure I must have hit some. Then I told him about the time when the Fifth Cavalry was with the whole command of General Crook and had to live on horse meat for nearly a month.

The captain shook his head, "You ate horse meat. I could not ever think about eating horses."

Other men were sitting close by. One man said, "It is true about eating horse meat, I have read in a small book about that war against the Sioux Indians. General Crook's men were out of food for several weeks and had to eat horse meat to stay alive."

The captain then said, "Well, you must have seen hard times. But you look so young to have been out in the wars."

"Young as I look," I said, "I was out on the campaign of starvation with General Crook and General Merritt."

"Well, sir," he said, "you have a great history behind you. Now get a good education and use it in the right way, so you can write a nice history about yourself and the things that you have seen. Now we are at our landing place. If I had the time, I would be very glad to go with you to General Merritt. But I must get back to the city by seven o'clock, and it is now almost noon. I must bid you farewell. I hope you have a good time with your old-time friend General Merritt. Mention my name." It is now so long ago that I have forgotten the name of that friendly man.

A young officer met me at the boat and went with me to General Merritt's quarters. A young colored woman appeared at the door, and the young officer told her that a young stranger wanted to see the general. The colored woman left the room, and soon a very large man appeared at the door. He quickly recognized me and called my name. "Why here is Mike," he said, "an Apache Fifth Cavalry boy."

I said, "General, I am happy to see you, sir."

The general turned to the officer, "Here is an Apache boy of my regiment, the Fifth Cavalry, who was captured by Captain James Burns and Lieutenant Earl Thomas in the year of 1872. Shake hands with Mike Burns."

In a few minutes, Mrs. Merritt came into the room. She also knew me at Fort Laramie before I came East to go to school in 1881.

After the general had eaten dinner, he went with me to the hotel to register my name for lodging, and I was shown my room. From the window I had a fine view of the Hudson River. Then we went back to his house and talked about old times—especially the 1876 campaign against the Sioux Indians when we crossed the Bad Lands and nearly starved to death.

At four o'clock, a fine black carriage arrived at the house. The driver was a black man dressed in a white suit and a shiny black hat. General and Mrs. Merritt and I sat in the carriage and the man drove us around the grounds where the cadets were parading. All the cadets saluted the carriage and me, too.

That night I ate a fine supper at the hotel and slept well all night. The next morning when I stepped out on the front porch of the hotel, a carriage was there waiting for me. The driver, the same driver as the night before, said that General Merritt wished me to come to his house. He seated me where the general had sat. The general who was waiting at his door showed me all around West Point. I saw cadets in their fine uniforms drilling to become soldiers or commanders of soldiers. At noon he took me back to the hotel, and after dinner the same carriage took me to the general's quarters.

General Merritt asked me lots of questions and at last he asked, "How would you like to be a cadet? In five years you can be an officer and be sent out to join a regiment where there is a vacancy." He told me to consider the matter carefully. He could enter me in the academy at once if I would choose to enter the place.

Such a fool I was, a young man who had not much sense. "No," I said, "I have so much to do at my school and on the farm, I cannot come to West Point." General Merritt then advised me to be sure to learn some trade or become a professor of some art.

General Merritt said no more about my education and asked, "Well when do you want to go back to the Valentine farm?" I said, "In the morning if the boat goes up to Newburgh."

He said, "The first boat goes up at seven o'clock."

I said, "I want to go up on the first boat."

He said, "Very well, I will make arrangements with the hotel. I will be at the depot to see you off."

I visited General Merritt in March 1883. I had a chance to become a West Point cadet and five years later a second lieutenant in an army regiment. I might have been sent out to an infantry, cavalry or artillery regiment—perhaps to Arizona to join the Sixth or Seventh Cavalry. I could have drawn a salary of one hundred twenty-five dollars a month instead of twenty-five dollars a month as a scout. After six months, I was discharged and out of a job and had nothing. Occasionally, I went out cutting wild gramma hay for the San Carlos agency at one cent a pound or wood for six dollars a cord. Sometimes, I had the good luck to get a job as an interpreter at two dollars and fifty cents a day.

I might have been an officer in the United States Army for thirty years and by now a high ranking officer. Again, I might have been killed in some war. I am glad that I have gone to a simple life even though I had to work hard to earn a living. I have always been happy and have had only minor illnesses.

I returned to Valentine's farm and stayed there until late April when I made up my mind to return to the Carlisle

School. First, I wanted to take in the sights along the Hudson River and visit New York City. So, I went up to Newburgh and got on the boat going to New Jersey—a distance of fifty-six miles or more. I had the same captain as before. He invited me to sit with him at the top of the boat where I could see all the beautiful scenery. He pointed out some places where battles were fought with British soldiers during the Revolutionary War. Near evening, I reached New Jersey, changed boats and crossed the bay.

I intended to see the sights of New York City that I had heard so much about. I did not see so much. It rained so hard that I walked only a few blocks and went into a hotel. I had the chance to see the great Brooklyn Bridge that was only half finished and saw some of the great ships going under the bridge and up the East River. I visited Brooklyn, but I could see nothing of interest to me. So I went back to New York City where I stayed two days. The whole time I was there I could not see anything, and I could not go anywhere. The streets and walks were so crowded I was often knocked over in the muddy streets. I could not enjoy such a place where it rained all the time. So I left New York and went again to Jersey City where I took a train to Philadelphia. I had in mind to see that city too, but it still rained and the fog set in, and I could not see much. I stayed one night in Philadelphia and the next morning was on a train bound for Harrisburg where I changed to a train going to Carlisle and Carlisle Indian School.

At the time of my return, about three hundred fifty students attended the school. While I was working on Valentine's farm, Captain Pratt had enrolled about fifty Cheyennes and Arapahos from the Darlington Agency near Fort Reno, Indian Territory and seventy-five Sioux from the Standing Rock Agency in South Dakota.

I did not stay long enough at the Carlisle Indian School to complete all their courses. I knew that no one could progress very fast going to classes for only half the day and doing little odd jobs the other half. I wished to go some place where I could go to school and study my lessons all day and work on Saturdays for wages and board.

Early in May 1883, Captain Pratt called me to his office. He had received a letter from a farmer in Ohio. The farmer and his wife wanted a young man who was a good worker and could speak the English language to live with them and work as a farm hand. Captain Pratt said he knew no other Indian boy who had a better knowledge of English and civilized life and who was also a good worker. He asked if I wanted to go out in the country where I could work all summer and go to school in the winter. I gladly accepted that offer.

Superintendent's Quarters, West Point, New York

28
Lore City, Ohio
May 1883 — September 1884

The next morning, Miss Robertson, the chief clerk of the Carlisle Indian School, and I were on the train to Harrisburg where we changed to one bound for Pittsburgh. This city was well known for its coal mining and iron works. It was so smoky and misty that I could not see the sun. I wanted to look around, but we did not have much time and Miss Robertson did not want to miss the next train. We rode all night along the Ohio River as far as Wheeling, West Virginia where we boarded a train on the Ohio Railroad going west.

I was expecting to see great buildings and many people at Lore City, Guernsey County, Ohio. When we arrived, I saw only three or four houses and a station. It was only a railroad station after all. Mr. and Mrs. Johnson met us with a wagon and a team and drove us to their home about three miles away. Mr. Johnson showed me a room where I could make my home, and Mrs. Johnson showed Miss Robertson a room they called a guest room.

Mr. Johnson took me to the barn where he kept three work horses and many milk cows. He asked me if I could milk a cow. I said I could. Then he asked if I could drive a team of horses. I said I could do almost any kind of farm work. Alvah Johnson said I was the kind of boy he wanted.

Miss Robertson saw right away that the Johnsons and I were well suited to one another. She stayed one night, wished me good luck and much success, bid me good bye, and returned to Carlisle Indian School.

I lived with a very fine, good-natured couple. Alvah Johnson had just married Lizzie Sprout. The Sprout family lived at a farm bordering the Johnsons'. They were all Christian people belonging to the Presbyterian Church. Mr. Sprout was the head elder of the church, and Mr. Johnson, the father of Alvah, was a trustee. Mr. McColluck from another adjoining farm was another church trustee.

Early on the morning after my arrival, Mr. Johnson and I were out in the wagon hauling in the hay he had already cut and raked the day before. He drove the wagon, and I loaded the hay on the wagon. He often remarked on how well I handled a pitch fork.

I soon learned what my work on the farm would be. Each evening I brought in the many cows from the meadows, and early every morning I milked them. The milk was taken by train to the city of Cambridge, Ohio twenty-five miles away. During hay season, Mr. Johnson drove the wagon, and I loaded on the hay. When plowing season came, I took out the team and plowed the ground.

In October I stopped working on the farm and went to school. The school house was four miles away. I walked to school with the white children—Lizzie Johnson, Alvah's fourteen-year-old sister; Mary Sprout, Lizzie's sister; and three children from the McColluck family. When it rained or snowed, Alvah took his sister Lizzie and me to school in the wagon. I learned quickly in this little country school, and no one treated me different because I was an Indian.

Each Sunday I went with the Johnsons and the Sprouts to the Presbyterian church, and during the week I often went to church meetings. I was surrounded all the time by good Christian people. So while I was getting a good education, I was also learning about Christianity. These good people advised me to study the Bible and go out West as a missionary to my people—to teach them the Gospel so that they might become good Indians and stop fighting other people. The Yavapais and Apaches never had anybody to tell them about God and his loving message.

I stayed with the Johnsons two summers and went to school one winter. I received a fair education and a good understanding of the English language. In one year attending the country school, I learned more than I would have in five years at Carlisle, Pennsylvania.

Early in August 1884, I wrote a letter to Captain Pratt asking him to erase my name from the enrollment at Carlisle. I was thinking about heading West and would hunt work on the way. I planned to save my wages and enter some other schools in winter.

I had received letters from Elwood Doran, a friend from the Carlisle school, inviting me to his home in Rulo, Nebraska on the Iowa, Sac and Fox Reservation. My friend wrote that there I could find plenty of work at three dollars and fifty cents for an eight hour day. This was the first place I had in mind to go.

Captain Pratt replied in a letter to Mr. Johnson that my agreement for a three year scholarship had expired. I was no longer enrolled at Carlisle, and I could do as I wished. I could go wherever I wanted at my own expense. The government would look after me no longer.

After reading the letter, Alvah Johnson said, "You have lived with me now nearly two years. I can say that your work has been most satisfactory, and the neighbors speak very highly about you. I am going to make you a proposal that I think is in your best interest for the future. If you choose to stay with me another year, there is a house and barn and about twenty-five acres you can have to start on. I know two nice looking girls, whom you have seen at meetings and fairs. They would be very happy to have you as a husband, and their parents would be pleased."

I now remember only the first names of the two girls I once knew in Guernsey County, Ohio. One was Lulu and the other was Annie.

Alvah's persuasion for me to stay on the farm was strong. But I had by this time made up my mind to go West in the direction of my old home. So I foolishly said, "Thank you. You are so kind and generous. You have taken me, an Indian boy, into your family. You are the most kindhearted people I have ever known. Now you make me an offer I find hard to refuse. But no, I must be going out West again where I belong. In that way I may some day reach my home in Arizona." I thought the land of my mother was more dear to me than the whole farm of Alvah Johnson and all the girls who lived near his home.

Alvah Johnson turned and looked sadly into his wife's face and said, "Well, Lizzie, I guess we have to lose Mike. I can not make him change his mind to stay. He insists on going West to his wild forests and deserts."

I was soon ready to go. Alvah Johnson had bought a trunk for me, and my few belongings were packed. I had saved about eighty-five dollars before coming to Lore City, and I was going out West on the railroad as far as the money went. When the money would be near the end, I intended to work at something for wages until I had enough money to ride again.

One fine morning, most of Alvah Johnson's neighbors including those two girls of my acquaintance went to the station to bid me good-bye. Alvah Johnson went into the ticket office. When he returned, he handed me a ticket "This," he said, "will take you as far as Atchison, Kansas, where I understand you want to go." He then handed me a large roll of greenbacks and smiled, "Here is two hundred seventy-five dollars for wages you have earned that I have saved for you. I hope you will make it last until you find another job."

Two hundred seventy-five dollars seemed like a lot of money to me who had never seen so much before in my life. I would not have had that much if Mr. Johnson had paid me wages every month. I was very much surprised. I never knew I was working for wages. He had given me board and room free even in the winter when I went to school and helped out only a little. Sometimes when I joined the family on pleasure trips, like the Ohio State Fair at Zaneville, he would give me three or five dollars to spend. When at last I swallowed the large lump in my throat, I could only say, "Thank you."

All the time Alvah was speaking, the two girls, Lulu and Annie, were holding my hands. I freed myself from the one on the right long enough to put the money into my pockets. I offered each of them five dollars, but they refused saying that I might need it in my travels and to keep it for their sakes. One of the girls—I think the one called Annie—sobbed bitterly, and I felt like doing the same.

When the train rolled into the station, I noticed that most of the women folks were tearful. I said, "Good-bye, you good people. You have treated me with much kindness all the time I have been with you. You all knew that I am of a different race, not a white man, but an Indian. You have treated me like one of your own people, like one of your own family. I will remember the friendship of the people in Lore City for the rest of my life."

29
Iowa, Sac and Fox Reservation and Highland Academy
September 1884 — April 1885

The train pulled out, and Lore City was soon out of sight. I tried to forget the faces of the kind people I had left at the station and to think of the new adventures ahead. I was on my way to Chicago, Illinois and then to Atchison, Kansas and finally to Rulo, Nebraska on the Iowa, Sac and Fox Reservation. Elwood Doran, my good friend from the Carlisle School, lived with his family on this reservation. He had often written letters to me while I was at Lore City and had asked me to come to his home. He wrote that hard working young Indians could get jobs at the agency, and he directed me how to get there.

After spending a day in Atchison looking around, I sent a telegram to the Indian agent at the Sac and Fox and Iowa reservation asking him to tell Elwood Doran to meet me at the station. Then I bought a ticket and took a train going up the Missouri River to Rulo.

Elwood met me at the Rulo Station about noon. Charles Kihiga, the chief's son, and several other Indians were with him. I thought some of these Indians acted rather strange. They had come with four wagons from their homes about fifteen miles away. When we were out on the road about four or five miles and had crossed the Meeneehaw River, someone called for the wagons to stop. One Indian drove his wagon into the thick brush, and the other four followed. When we all got out, the leader put a large keg of beer on the ground, pulled the stopper out, poured the beer into cups and gave one to each person. The women had drinks too. They emptied the barrel in a short time. By then the men who were acting strange in town were very drunk. I had just come from a good Presbyterian community where getting drunk is forbidden. I also knew that Indians were not allowed to drink beer or liquor on reservations. I did not join them in their drinking.

I learned that these Indians could obtain beer and whiskey from some half-breeds who could get it as easily as white men. Each Indian put in several dollars. Beer was the favorite drink among the Sac and Fox and Iowa Indians.

We got to Elwood Doran's home about midnight. The next morning, he took me around the reservation, which is only eight miles long and four miles wide. The land is very flat with no hills. All the people live in frame houses. Only two tribes, the Sac and Fox and the Iowas, live there. They had all lived for many years in Iowa until the white settlers forced Chief Kihiga of the Sac and Fox to sell all their lands. The tribe moved to the Indian reservation on the Kansas and Nebraska border. Later the Iowas joined them. Elwood belonged to the Iowa tribe.

After he showed me all there was to see, Elwood took me to the agency headquarters to meet the man who did the hiring. The agent said that the school needed repairs, and he thought that Elwood and I could do the work. The government wage was two dollars and fifty cents a day plus board. We accepted his offer, and the following day we moved to the agency so we could be near our place of work.

Elwood Doran and I started right away to fix up the school building. There was much to be done. We found the roof full of holes, broken windows, no doors and hardly any floor. We had worked together doing carpentry and painting at Carlisle, so we were used to working right along without stopping. First we climbed up on the roof, took off all the old shingles and put on new ones. After we got the building in good shape, we had to paint it. We were at this job a little over a month. Some days we did not work because of bad weather. When we were finished, we went to the agency to be paid. The agent said we each had seventy-five dollars coming, but the money had not come yet so we had to wait a few weeks more to be paid.

Meanwhile, some missionaries from Highland, Kansas, about twenty-seven miles away preached the Gospel to a small gathering of young Indians. One preacher often told me about a fine school in Highland. There was a good chance, he said, that I could enter Highland Presbyterian Academy. A young man like me with a good moral character would have no trouble being admitted there. I told this young Christian man if he would take me to Highland, I would try to enter the school. He agreed to take me to the university and introduce me to the president, Professor McCarty.

The young missionary took me to see the school president. "Why do you want to come to Highland Academy?" Professor McCarty asked.

"I want to attend Highland Academy," I said, "because I need to learn more so I can have a good profession. I want to be a school teacher."

He asked me what I had studied. I told him all about my schooling in Fort Laramie with the children of the officers and soldiers, how General Merritt had arranged for me to go to the Carlisle Indian school and of the little country schools in New York and Ohio.

Professor McCarty said that I had completed all the courses needed to enter the normal school. Then he gave me the books to study, mostly mathematics and physical geography, for the courses required for a teaching certificate. Late in October 1884, I entered Highland Presbyterian Academy. I had nearly three hundred dollars when I was enrolled. The tuition was twenty dollars a month, my board and room was twenty dollars, and I had to buy books. All the time I stayed at the school, it cost me over forty dollars a month without spending money in any foolish way as I was a young Christian man attending a highly respected Christian college.

I was the only Indian boy going to this school. Several years earlier, Presbyterian missionaries had established a mission school for the Sac and Fox and Iowa Indians, but these Indians were not interested in learning anything—only drinking beer and having a good time. I always told everybody I was an Apache Indian, because that was the only kind of Arizona Indian they had heard of. After three months, I left my white classmates behind, and in the next term I entered a higher class. Two months later, I was promoted to another grade leaving the others in my class far behind. Each time I went higher, I had to buy another set of books.

Professor McCarty often made me stand up. Then he told the other students how quickly I was going with my studies. He said that the other young men and women in his classes, who had learned English when they were babies and whose parents were all educated, were slow to learn their lessons. "Mike Burns," he said, "is an Apache Indian whose parents never spoke English and never saw a school. A few years ago, even Mike could not speak the language. He has been here only a few months and now he has surpassed all of you in your studies. Next year, he can go into any academic department he chooses. If he only wants to be a school teacher, I am willing at the end of this term to give him a license so he can teach in schools in Kansas."

Many Christian men and women had often said if I would listen to them and take their advice, they would help me in anything I wanted. I had taken some courses in the law and had some thoughts of becoming a lawyer. Those Christian good talkers promised me many things if I would give up studying law. They said that law was not an honorable profession, that no lawyers ever made an honest living. Lawyers always scheme to deprive people of their money, which is the same as stealing. These good Christians told me to change my course of study to religion, and they promised to help me in all things needed to get an education. "When you get such a degree," they said, "we will send you out West to your people—especially the Apaches who are always at war with other people. You can then teach them how to live right, to throw away their weapons, to stop fighting and live in peace because God does not want his people to kill one another. Then you will live well and not want for anything. Ask for it and you will get it."

So although I was much interested in studying law, I gave it up to study the Bible, and I went to all the church and missionary meetings.

I had to pay all my tuition fees and board in advance. By the end of April, I could not meet the required amount. To finish the term that ended in June, I needed ninety dollars more. I called on the church members for a loan of ninety dollars so I could finish the normal course. Professor McCarty had assured me that he would give me a certificate so that I could teach. Then I could easily return the amount of the loan. The pastor said, "The trustees of the church will meet on May 15. Then if they agree to lend you the money, I will surely approve it."

I needed the money right then. I had only twenty dollars to my name, and it cost me at least forty dollars a month to stay at the Highland Presbyterian Academy. So I then came to the conclusion that most all supposed Christian men and women make promises that they cannot fulfill. They make all kinds of talk. They say they will pray for you and will help at any time. I was in great need so I could obtain a thorough education and return to my homeland and help my people. I would have repaid the loan in a short time. As I left the pastor's house I said, "I will quit you church people, and from now on you will never see me in any church."

I went to the president's office and explained my circumstances. I told him that I must leave and look for work in the southern part of the state.

Professor McCarty said, "Mr. Burns, can you get any money at all?"

I explained, "The church members promised to give me help at any time. But now I know I must wait here until May 15 for the church trustee's decisions. After I wait here all that time, they may not agree to give me that amount. So I might as well go out and find work as soon as possible."

"Well," the professor said, "do not get too discouraged, my young man. Go back to school again when you can. You now have a good education. I will give you a teacher's certification. Just present it to school officials, and they will find a place for you. You have gone up very fast in your studies, and while you were going ahead, you left your white classmates far behind." So Professor McCarty gave me some letters and a teaching certificate to take with me wherever I went.

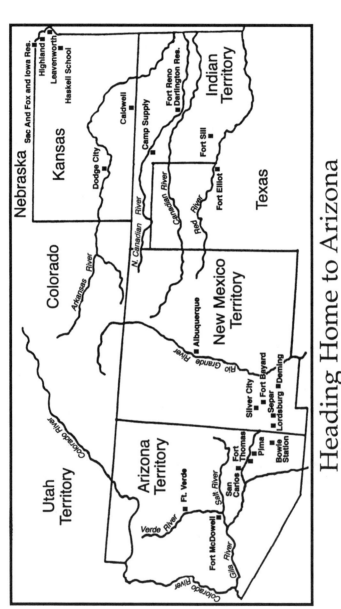

Heading Home to Arizona
April to December 1885

Part V

Mike Scouts
His Way Home
April to December 1885

30
Cowboys and Indian Scouts
April 1885 – October 1885

From Highland Academy I took a stage to the railroad depot about four miles away. Before I boarded the train, I sent a telegraph to Major John Upham, an old friend from the Fifth United States Cavalry. I told him I was out of school, short of money and out to hunt work. I asked him to pick me up, if he could, at the station in Leavenworth.

I had last seen Major Upham at the Red Cloud Agency in October 1876. That was nearly ten years earlier when I was still a young boy; now I was a young man. I knew from a recent letter from Lieutenant Bishop that Major Upham was at Fort Leavenworth enlisting men to go out West. Bishop told me if I ever got to Leavenworth to be sure to look him up, that he would be glad to see me. I hoped he would remember me. I need not have worried. As soon I stepped off the train at Leavenworth, Major Upham came to me, shook my hand and led me to his carriage a short distance away. A driver put my little trunk and my bundle of blankets into the carriage and took us to Upham's house where I stayed a few days.

Major Upham took me to the places where the soldiers drilled. I recognized some men from the campaign of 1876 with General Crook. When Major Upham took me to target practice, he proposed that we shoot too. He told the soldiers that I had fought with him in the Sioux War in 1876. The target was placed at about three hundred yards. The major shot three times and hit the target once. He handed me the gun. The first shot hit near the bull's eye, the second hit the edge of the bull's eye and the third was a little high. I did better than Major Upham who said, "Mike, you can still shoot." I had not shot a weapon for nearly nine years.

One officer said, "If he comes out to practice every day like the soldiers, he can beat Major Carver. Better yet, send him to the front."

That night, I had champagne and dinner at Major Upham's house. The next morning, I told him that I was going to Lawrence to work at the hay harvest for a month. If I should find a steady job, I might stay longer. I promised to let him know if I decided to return to Leavenworth. He said, "By all means let me hear from you. If you have no success in finding work, let me know. There is some talk of hiring a large number of Indian scouts, and I would be willing to get you in."

Before I left his house, Major Upham handed me a twenty dollar bill; "If you do not find work soon," he said, "this will help until you do. Be sure to write as soon as you get to Lawrence."

Three days after my arrival in Lawrence, I met a man who wanted a farm worker. I said I would try him out, and if I suited him I might stay longer. For three days, I raked hay and stacked it close to the barn. Then I helped harvest corn. I stayed at this farm only three weeks.

The Haskell United States Indian School was a few miles from the town of Lawrence, so I made a visit. The superintendent of the school wanted to enroll me as a student. But I said, "I will enter this school, not as a student, but as a teacher."

The superintendent said, "I cannot enroll an Indian first entering the school as a teacher." I showed him the certificate that Professor McCarty had given me and tried to tell him that I was qualified to be a teacher anywhere in the state of Kansas where there was an opening. "Well," he said, "I will have to contact the headquarters for Indian Schools in Washington."

Knowing that it might be several years before he heard from Washington, I said, "Well, if you have to go to all that trouble, I will be on my way as I am also a laborer."

I returned to Lawrence, took the train to Leavenworth and went to see Major Upham. He said, "Some recruits are about to drive many horses and mules from Caldwell, Kansas to Fort Reno, Indian Territory. I think you can go with them. When you get to Reno, you can enlist as a scout in the United States Army. Many scouts are needed in Indian Territory."

Major Upham took me to the office of General Nelson Miles, the commander of the Department of Missouri. This was my first meeting ever with General Miles. It would not be my last. He was a great general and was very helpful to me. General Miles gave me a letter authorizing me as an employee of the United States government to drive cattle from Caldwell to Fort Reno. He gave me another letter for the commanding officer at Fort Reno recommending me as a scout. Major Upham then arranged my transportation to Caldwell.

I arrived by freight train at Caldwell just in time to spend the following three days herding horses to Fort Reno. About the time I reached Fort Reno, several Cheyennes and Arapahos arrived there from the Darlington Agency about three miles away. Some came to enlist as scouts and others just tagged along. I noticed that all the time they talked to one another, they kept looking at me.

The next morning, as I was walking to the headquarters to enlist as a scout, an Arapaho Indian in a buggy drove up to me and asked me to come to his camp and visit his people. I agreed and was taken to a lodge where many old men and women were seated. As I entered, they raised their heads to look at me, and as I came closer many began to cry. Then one Indian explained that it was about thirteen years since they had seen me. At that time the United States soldiers fought them and captured many of their children. They said that I was one of the captured children. One old woman came to me and felt my ears and found a hole that she said had been pierced by her daughter when I was a baby. The daughter was killed during the fight when I was taken. The old woman said she was my grandmother.

I knew I was not a long lost relative of these good people. I had to explain who I was, where I had come from and what I was doing at Fort Reno. I told them that I had learned to speak many Arapaho words at Fort Brown, Wyoming in 1878, and I had learned the sign language well. So when I met them at Fort Reno and spoke a few words of their language, they began to believe I was one of their people. I was captured almost exactly the same time that the boy from their tribe was captured.

All the time I was in that large lodge surrounded by so many friendly men and women, I kept thinking about getting out of there. I needed to be back at the fort in time to be enlisted.

There was much excitement on the Reno post. The soldiers had heard reports that cowboys of all kinds— Mexicans, half breeds, and a very rough class of white men from Texas, New Mexico and southern Arizona—were making problems for the government. The cattlemen had started the trouble by cutting a wire fence that enclosed an area about eight miles wide. They drove about sixty thousand cattle straight across Indian Territory to Kansas City instead of taking the route through Dodge City. When the Darlington agent heard this, he sent several Indian policemen to the cattlemen with orders not to run their cattle through Indian Territory. But the head boss tore up the orders and threatened to shoot the Indians on the spot if they did not hurry back in the direction from which they came. The Indian police reported that at least five thousand cattlemen had gathered in the area, defying the government and shooting at the Indians. The agent asked soldiers from Fort Reno to escort the Indian policemen to confront the cattlemen. The cattlemen forced the soldiers and policemen back to the post. The commanding officer of Fort Reno then sent reports to General Miles at his headquarters in Fort Leavenworth and to the War Department about the cattlemen defying the government forces. He requested the assistance of a few regiments of cavalry and five hundred or more Indian scouts.

There were no objections to my enlistment as I had letters from General Miles and Major Upham at headquarters. I was to be sent out with one hundred fifty scouts and five hundred soldiers. The pay was twenty-five dollars a month plus rations and horse food. Three hundred scouts had already gone out, and more soldiers were expected to arrive at Fort Reno at any time. I reported to Lieutenant Sedgewick Rice who was in charge of fifty Cheyenne and Arapaho scouts. Lieutenant Rice wanted a young man to tend to his horse and fix up his place. For the extra work he would pay me fifteen dollars a month. Lieutenant Rice then sent me to the post surgeon for a physical examination. After looking me over, Dr. McNara gave me a paper to take to the post commander, Captain Connell, who signed my enlistment paper. I was once again a scout in the United States Army.

Lieutenant Rice ordered the company of fifty scouts to get ready to march in the morning up the Canadian River to

Cantonment and to Camp Supply. I had no horse so I had to make haste to get one. I asked around if any Indian wanted to sell a pony. A school mate of mine from Carlisle, a Cheyenne boy named Tom Roberts, sold me a horse for twenty-five dollars, and I bought a secondhand saddle and a pistol at the trader's store. I spent over fifty dollars before I left Fort Reno.

We rode for three long days to reach Camp Supply. I recognized much of the country although it was nearly ten years since I left there to go north to fight the Sioux. We stayed there two days before continuing our four-day march south to Fort Elliot, Texas. Because Lieutenant Rice did not come along, I worked for Lieutenant Blackburn who took over the command.

After we had been stationed about four weeks at Fort Elliot, the commanding officer received a telegram from Fort Reno. Three hundred fifty Indians were reported to be away from their homes on the Darlington Reservation and were making their way south down the Arkansas River toward Fort Sill. Lieutenant Blackburn ordered his Indian scouts to scout out in an easterly direction toward Fort Sill. After scouting for two days in the direction of Fort Reno and about fifty miles from Fort Elliot, we came upon one hundred fifty lodges of Cheyennes and Arapahos. About seven hundred people were away from their reservation. We escorted them to Fort Elliot, the nearest post.

For the next few days, Major Anson Mills, the post commander tried to find the reason for the Indians' departure from the Darlington Reservation. Was it to fight soldiers or to steal animals? Mills could not find a single Cheyenne who could interpret for his people. Finally, Lieutenant Blackburn asked me if I could speak the Cheyenne language. I said I could not talk to them right out, but I understood the motion of their hands. I could talk to them in sign language. Blackburn decided that would do.

Major Mills called me to his office in the headquarters building. We recognized each other at once. "You are the little Indian boy who accompanied Lieutenant Bishop everywhere during the Big Horn and Yellowstone Campaign. You are now grown into a man," he said.

"Yes, I am Mike Burns," I said. "You are the officer who led the attack on the Cheyenne village at Slim Buttes, and the rest of us had to hurry up to help you out." He asked me what I had been doing, and I told him how I had been East getting an education and learning the ways of white people.

"Do you think you can find out why the Cheyennes left their reservation?" Major Mills asked.

"I will do my best," I said.

Chief Crazy Mule met with Major Mills and me at the headquarters building. I asked the chief why he was away from his reservation without permission. He said he was out to hunt deer, antelope and buffalo for food for the coming winter. He had not harmed anyone while he was out. "If I had been on the war path," he said, "I would have killed everyone in the party that found us."

Major Mills said he would report all that Crazy Mule had said to General Miles at his headquarters in Leavenworth. However, Crazy Mule and his people must go back to the reservation. Twenty-five soldiers and fifteen scouts escorted the Cheyennes back to Fort Reno. I did not go with them.

A few days later, I joined a company that was to make certain no more cattle came to Indian Territory from Texas. If the cattlemen should insist on driving their cattle across the reservation, we were told to hold the men and cattle under guard.

Every morning before the sun was up, the scouts went out to gather the ponies and feed them corn or barley. We crossed bottom lands where the grass grew higher than a man's head. It was fall, and the dew was very heavy. Our clothes became as wet as if we had walked through water. Many of us suffered from colds. I was worse off than anyone else in the camp and was sent to Fort Elliot for treatment. I stayed around the post on the sick list taking medicine every morning. It seems that the more medicine I took, the worse my cough got. I concluded that the medicine was no good for such a bad cold. I knew the Indians had herbs that in most cases would cure coughs in a few days.

News arrived at Fort Elliot that Geronimo and several Chiricahua Apaches had broken out of San Carlos. They had killed a white man, an Indian police sergeant and several people in the settlements around San Carlos. They were hiding out in Mexico or Texas. General Crook was ordered back to Arizona to command the soldiers against Geronimo and the Chiricahua Apaches.

While I was just sitting around on the sick list with nothing to do, I wrote a long letter to my old friend, General George Crook, who was stationed at Fort Bowie, Arizona. I wrote him how I was in a low, damp country with a people who were strangers to me. I had such a very hard cough, and when I spoke, no one at any distance could hear me. I feared if I stayed in this place three or four months more, my days on earth would end here. I asked him to use his influence to transfer me to the Department of Arizona. As he well knew, I wrote, I belonged to the Apache-Mohave people and not to the Cheyennes or Arapahos. I did not belong in this Eastern country. I told him I wanted to return to my mother's land.

Less than three weeks after I sent the letter to General Crook, a telegram came to Major Anson Mills who called me to his office. Major Mills had orders from General Crook for me to go to Fort Leavenworth. Major Mills said I should sell all the stuff I had at the camp. When I got everything in good shape, the guartermaster would arrange my

transportation to Fort Leavenworth. I was to   report to
General Nelson Miles, the commander of the Department of
the Missouri.

I sold my horse and saddle for twenty-five dollars, but
I had loaned the pistol I had bought for fifteen dollars at
Fort Reno to Lieutenant Blackburn for him to carry on a
trip. The quartermaster said that after I was settled, I should
write to him and give him my address. He would let Lieutenant Blackburn know that I wanted my pistol or fifteen
dollars.

Two days later when I arrived by stage at Camp Supply, I was surprised to see my old fatherly friend Captain
Hall Bishop. I had to leave on another stage the next morning, but I stayed over night with him at his quarters. We had
written a few times, but we had not seen each other for five
years. We both had changed. He was married now, and he
and his wife, Theresa, had two little children. We sat up
most of the night talking about old times—especially about
the time we were together in the Sioux War. We knew we
might never meet again, but we agreed to write to one another. Early the next morning, he took me to the post
where the stage was waiting. Bishop took hold of my hand
and said, "Be good, my boy, perhaps we may never meet
again. Be good as long as you may live. Good-bye my
boy."

After the stage had crossed the river and was over the
hills about six miles away, I looked back and saw the valleys
of both Beaver and Wolf Creeks that joined to make the
Canadian River. I came to the conclusion that the mind of a
man changes, but the land never changes.

We traveled all day and all night, stopping only to
change horses, covering about ninety-five miles. The stage
rolled into the Dodge City station about nine in the morning. Before boarding the train going east, I telegraphed my
friend Major Upham. I changed trains again at Kansas City,

and it was but a short trip to Leavenworth. Major Upham met me at the depot and took me to his quarters.

That night I slept soundly for the first time in nearly six months. In the morning Upham took me to the office of General Miles. After bidding us to come in and be seated, General Miles pulled out a letter written to him by General Crook from Camp Bowie, Arizona. "Is it true you want to be transferred from this department to Arizona?" he asked.

I said, "Yes, sir."

"Where do you want to go?"

"I have been away from my people for over ten years. I want to go home."

"Where is your home?"

"Arizona, at the San Carlos Agency."

"Well young man," he said, "I can send you only as far as my department extends—that is to Fort Bayard, New Mexico. From there you can join some scouting parties going after the Chiricahuas and in that way join General Crooks' command and then somehow get to San Carlos."

"Thank you, sir. That is just what I was hoping," I said, "The plan should work out well for me."

"Very well," General Miles said, "be ready to leave in the morning. The quartermaster will have the papers ready for you travel on to Fort Bayard. You will go from here to Kansas City where you will change to a train going west to Albuquerque and Deming. You will again change trains to Silver City, where you will be able to find an ambulance going to Fort Bayard. There you will report to the commanding officer for duty."

The next day I boarded the Southern Pacific headed for New Mexico. I was on my way home at last.

31
Going Home
October — December 1885

Two days later I arrived at Silver City, New Mexico, a rough mining town with more saloons than houses. Many soldiers were hanging about the depot. I walked up to one wearing a sergeant's uniform. "How can I get to Fort Bayard?" I asked.

The sergeant asked, "Are you Mike Burns?" Surprised that he knew my name, I just nodded and said, "Yes."

"You are the man I am looking for. My men and I are here to take you to Fort Bayard in that light wagon yonder." He pointed to the nearby ambulance to which four mules were hitched.

One soldier helped me load my gear into the wagon, and the sergeant said, "We need not be in any hurry as we have all day to ourselves. We can have a little fun around this town until about four o'clock and then we'll be on our way. It is only nine miles to the fort, and we can get there in less than two hours easily."

I did not want to seem ungrateful, and I did not have a choice anyway. I thought, 'Why not, it has been a long time since I had some pleasure.' I just said, "Sure, I'd like to have a little fun."

We went first to a pool hall. I was pretty good at pool as I had played at many posts. I played a few games with the soldiers and beat them at almost every game. The sergeant said, "There is a quartermaster sergeant at the post, we would like to see you beat." Later, I played the quartermaster sergeant and I lost.

At four o'clock, the sergeant, the six soldiers and I were on our way. As we rode along in the ambulance, I noticed that the six soldiers kept their hands on their guns. "We must always be on the lookout for hostile Indians," the sergeant said. "Two weeks ago four miners were killed just a few miles from Silver City. So every man must keep his hand on his gun."

"I am sorry if you boys are taking a big chance on my account," I said. "I just want to say that although I am an Indian, I have enlisted in the United States Army to fight hostile Indians, and that is my intention." I wished then that I had the gun that I had loaned to Lieutenant Blackburn.

Then the sergeant said, "I was ordered this morning to take a wagon and six soldiers to Silver City and meet a soldier coming in on a train. Soldiers have to obey orders no matter what may befall them."

We arrived at Fort Bayard about six o'clock in the afternoon. I was shown to vacant quarters in the company to which I was assigned for duty. Only one company of infantry and one of cavalry remained at the post to protect it from outlaws. Most of the companies were out scouting for Geronimo and his band of warriors.

The next morning the sergeant who brought me from Silver City took me to the adjutant's office. The adjutant then took me to the commanding officer. "This is Mike Burns," he said. "He is an Apache Indian scout on his way to the San Carlos Agency in Arizona."

The commander did no look up from his desk. "Why has he come to Fort Bayard all by himself without a company?" he asked.

The adjutant replied, "He is here by order of General Miles, the commander of the Department of the Missouri."

"Oh, then," said the commander, finally looking at me, "you can stay here until some scouting duties come up. Some Apache scouts will be coming from the south soon, and when they come you will join them."

So I went to the barracks of the company to which I had been assigned, and stayed there about three weeks waiting further orders. There was no one else there, so I just slept and ate there all by myself until a few men came in and took up their old bunks. One old soldier made his bed right next to mine. No one noticed that he was very sick and might die at any moment. No one noticed that the man made no sound during the whole night. We woke about six o'clock and ate our breakfast. But the man who was sleeping next to me did not show up for breakfast. The cook was mad because he had to cook again for just one more. So he hurried into the room shouting at the man, but the man did not hear him. He went to the man's bed, uncovered his blanket and shook his face. He decided that the man must be dead. He called to the others who ran to the bed and agreed that he was soundly dead.

The company sergeant reported that one of his men who had just come in from the field had died that night from unknown causes. That afternoon there was a funeral. I had seen many men—white men and Indians—die, but this was the first time I ever saw a man just fall asleep and never wake up.

The very next day a miner rushed into the camp yelling and demanding to see the post commander. He reported that an Indian party had come into a little mining town north of the post. The Indians, the man said, had killed three men, driven off several animals, burned some buildings and were still shooting when he escaped. The commanding officer ordered the cavalry company that had just arrived and me to see what the Indians had done.

In about an hour, a lieutenant, fifty men and I began our march through the mountains. We passed through several peaceful towns, and in a few hours we reached a place called Miners' Pass. It had only a few buildings, and nearly every one was a saloon. Some soldiers dropped out of line and bought a few bottles of beer and whiskey. When we reached the bottom of the mountain, the command made camp by a little stream.

That night several soldiers starting drinking their beer and whiskey, and pretty soon they began to fight among themselves. Some went to get their guns, which were quickly taken from them. The next morning their horses were also taken from them, and they had to walk.

We started out bright and early and soon arrived at the place where—we had been told—Indians had attacked. Many buildings had been burned to the ground; others were still smoking. We marched into the center of town. Several men stood right in the middle of the road waiting for us. As we approached them, they pointed their guns at us.

Our lieutenant shouted, "Do not shoot. We have come here to protect you."

One big fellow who seemed to be in charge said, "We are ready to shoot anybody who comes into our town as we have been attacked often here."

"Who do you supposed did it?" the lieutenant asked, "Were they really Indians?"

"Well," the man said, "they must have been Indians because who else would have done this to white people."

"About what time did the attackers leave?" the lieutenant asked.

"Well sir," said the miner, "this all happened yesterday morning early, and the parties went over yonder." He pointed to the northeast.

So the lieutenant ordered his men to head out in that direction and told me to go ahead of the column. I soon found the horses' tracks and showed them to the lieutenant.

"These are the tracks of seven horses," I said. "They are wearing iron shoes. Indian ponies never have iron shoes." We followed the tracks about three miles, then came to a stream of water where the renegade parties had halted.

We followed a creek upstream through a pine-covered valley. We passed many ranches that seemed be undisturbed by any trouble. When the commander ordered us to stop, I thought he must have noticed Indians in the distance. The officer called to me, "Go a little ways up the hillside and see what is up ahead. It looks like an Indian or perhaps a bear standing on its hind feet waiting for us."

So with my gun in hand and prepared to shoot in a moment, I climbed the hill, peeked through some brush and could see clearly that a bear was waiting for us. I approached the animal cautiously. When I was close enough to hit it, I could see that the old bear was really only the stump of a burned down pine tree. I motioned for the men to proceed.

As we came to a cattle ranch, a man appeared with a gun in his hand. Our commander asked if he knew anything about Chiricahuas raiding through the valley. The man said that there had been no raids, but farther up the valley some miners and cowboys had been fighting. He said he would not expect any trouble from Chiricahuas this far north because they did not know the country or the water holes.

We passed many deserted ranches. At one ranch four men with pistols appeared. They had heard of no Indian raids, but they reported that about six cowboys had come racing their horses through the ranch and in every direction, firing their pistols and nearly killing some of the ranch hands. They had ridden off toward the hills. The lieutenant soon concluded that the men reporting depredations by the Indians had themselves attacked the poor prospectors to scare them off. Geronimo and his Chircahuas were down in Mexico nearly two hundred fifty miles away. Since there was no use looking for hostile Indians, we marched back the way we had come toward Fort Bayard.

In late November, a messenger reported that Apaches had killed six soldiers near the little town of Lourdsburg situated on the Southern Pacific Railroad about thirty-five miles west of Separ. All soldiers and scouts from Fort Bayard were ordered to the front. We moved out that afternoon and camped just below Silver City. The soldiers did not go into town to get whiskey and behaved well all day and night. The next morning we were on the desert roads riding toward the railroad.

Soon after our arrival at the railroad station at Separ, a company of soldiers and five Apache scouts came in from the mountains where they had been watching the movement of the hostiles. Soon after that a train rolled in from El Paso in southwestern Texas bringing more soldiers and twenty-five Tonto scouts returning to San Carlos. Lieutenant Ship, who was in charge of all the scouting detachments, ordered the company I had accompanied from Fort Bayard on a scout into the nearby mountains—and me with them. I said that I was supposed to go with the scouts returning to the San Carlos Agency so that I could be discharged there. Lieutenant Ship said to do as he had ordered.

So I went to the telegraph office and sent a telegram to General Crook. I asked him to reply at once as I had only a little over a month to serve, and this might be my only chance to get on a train going to Fort Bowie.

Two hours later I received a telegram from General Crook directing me to go with the Tonto scouts to Bowie

Station and on to San Carlos. When I showed the telegram to Lieutenant Ship, he told me to go where I wanted, and I was soon on the train with the Tonto-Apache scouts. I could only talk with those who spoke English. I was just as bad off as a white man with these Indians.

At Bowie station, the Tonto scouts prepared for their trip to San Carlos. The officer in charge told me to load my things on the train going to Fort Bowie. I tried to make him understand that I was on my way to San Carlos where I was to remain until my discharge. But he ordered me to Fort Bowie, and I was in the same fix I had been at Separ. So I quickly found the telegram from General Crook authorizing me to travel with the Tonto scouts to San Carlos. I handed the telegram to the officer in charge. After he read it, he gave me a note authorizing me six days rations and told me to proceed to San Carlos. I gave the note to the sergeant who was in charge of the trip.

The company moved out on foot. But before the station was out of sight, I noticed a little old two-mule wagon that carried the grub and other stuff for the scouts. I told the sergeant that I was a cavalry scout and not much used to traveling by foot. He was a kindhearted fellow and glad to meet an Indian who spoke such good English, so we got into the wagon and sat on top of the load together.

After traveling through a nearly barren desert for two days, we arrived at Solomonville on the Gila River where I saw many farmhouses and barns. It was December so most of the trees had lost their leaves and the horses and cows grazed in brown meadows. The place looked more like the farmlands in the East than what I remembered about Arizona.

The next day we traveled along the Gila River about twenty-two miles toward a little town called Pima. The sergeant warned the Tontos not to stray far from the wagon because the Mormons would shoot them. Near Pima,

Geronimo had crossed the river, shot many white men, and run off several herds of horses. Now, these Mormons looked at all Indians—Tontos, Apache-Yumas, Apache-Mohaves or Coyoteros—the same. They were all Chiricahuas to them. But some foolish scouts disobeyed and went on ahead. Many white men came with their guns and shot at them. The scouts ran quickly back to the wagon, and the sergeant explained the facts to them. The sergeant said that they should know by now that most white settlers in the Southwest are deadly enemies of the Apaches and will want to shoot any Indian they see.

So the Tontos marched close to the wagon until we reached Fort Thomas where we got the rations we needed for the rest of our journey. The reservation line was close to Fort Thomas, and the Indians knew that on the reservation they were no longer in danger from the Mormons—only from Chiricahuas coming to steal women from other Indian tribes. We followed the Gila to a deserted settlement and set up camp where the wagon road crosses the river going to Fort Apache. At midnight most of the Tontos left the camp and headed for the agency twenty-two miles away without the escort.

I had strange and mixed feelings as I traveled across the San Carlos Reservation. Memories of my childhood raced through my head. I recalled the last sight of my dear old grandfather on the morning I left my cave home, never to return, never to see any of my family again. I then remembered that terrible night before my capture—the night when I nearly froze to death. I thought of Captain Burns' kindness and the horrible massacre of all my family in the bloody cave on the Salt River. It was nearly thirteen years since I had been at San Carlos—the time I ran away from Captain Burns to join my people.

"What would my life have been like," I asked myself, "if I had not returned that night to Captain Burns and the

Fifth Cavalry?" I might never have left Arizona and seen so
much of the world. I would not have learned to speak such
good English or to read and write so well. I had learned
useful trades at the Carlisle Indian School and studied to be
a teacher at Highland Academy. I had so many opportuni-
ties. I could have gone to West Point and become an army
officer or I might have been a farmer in Ohio with a pretty
white wife. All the times were not so good. I nearly starved
to death in the Sioux Wars and was almost captured by
Cheyenne Indians. Tears came to my eyes as I thought of
my rescue by Lieutenant Bishop. I had so many good
friends in the United States Army, and I would think about
them often. But after my arrival at the Carlisle School, I
only wanted to get a good education and return to Arizona
and my people.

"Will I know anyone?" I asked myself. "Will anyone
recognize me? Ten years ago when I left Arizona on my big
adventure, I was a little boy about ten years old. Now I am
a grown man. Will anyone be glad to see me? How will I
support myself after I am discharged from the army?"

About two in the afternoon the sergeant with whom I
was riding pointed to a tented camp and said, "There is the
San Carlos agency." I had not returned to the land of my
people, but I had returned to the place where my people
lived.

Part VI

Mike at San Carlos
1885 — 1897

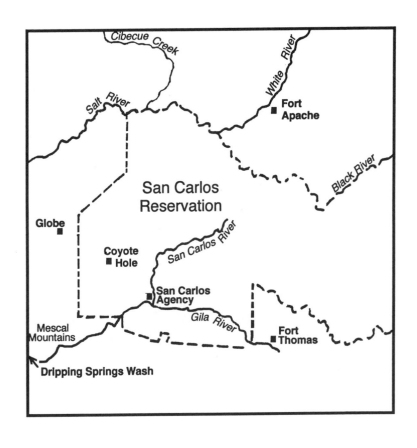

San Carlos
1885-1897

Mike Burns, U. S. Army Scout, About 1885
Photo from M. C. Hepler Collection

32
San Carlos
December 1885 — May 1887

When we reached the headquarters of the San Carlos agency, my sergeant kindly arranged for me to draw my rations allowance with a white detachment of the Eleventh Infantry, the company of Captain Edwin Pierce, the acting Indian agent at the San Carlos Agency. I unloaded my little bundle into a tent near a large wall tent that served as the soldiers' dining room. I was very surprised to find the United States Army still living in tents much like the one that Captain Burns and I had slept in twelve years earlier

While I was signing in at the headquarters, a young Indian came up to me. He recognized me and called me by name. "Mike Burns," he said, "I think I remember you as Hoomothya." I was greatly surprised. I had not heard the name my mother gave me since the happy days at Date Creek Camp when Mrs. Corbusier always called me by my Indian name. This young Indian's name was Quak-ni-due-yah (Summer Deer). He was a cousin. He must have had a great memory to remember me because we had been separated since we were small children. He also had been to the Carlisle School a year or so after I had left for Ohio, and he returned to San Carlos as James Roberts. His parents had been killed by the Pimas and Maricopas when he was but a baby. Older relatives had rescued him and had taken him to our village where he grew up. I was not so lonely now that I had met someone from my people, a young man I had known in the past. As we left the headquarters building, many Indians—men, women and children—were gathering nearby. James Roberts said they were Apache-Mohaves—the tribe I belonged to—preparing for a war dance. I thought as I looked them over that they seemed as much like Indians on the warpath as they had at the time of my capture in December 1872. I recognized no one, and no one knew me. However, many looked at me, and I believe they asked among themselves who I was. As I walked among them, I realized I could not understand a word they were saying. In all the years I had been gone from my homeland, I had not heard or spoken a word of my own language. I had served as an interpreter with the Arapahos and Cheyennes and other Indians; but with my own people I needed an interpreter. I asked James Roberts to explain all that was happening.

James Roberts said about one hundred fifty Tontos, Apache-Mohaves, Apache-Yumas, and San Carlos Apaches had just enlisted as scouts to hunt down Geronimo. The Apache-Mohave scouts were going out in the field the next day, and it was customary to have a war dance before they left the camp. The Apache-Mohaves believed that such a celebration would bring them luck in battle. I had not seen a dance performed by my people for many years and eagerly looked forward to seeing it.

Soon after dark, the people collected around the campfires. The men were naked except for breechcloths around their bodies and feathers on their heads. Those with drums stood in the center. Some danced forward and back, and others ran around in circles. The women danced in between the men. They kept up the dance nearly all night. Just before daylight, the scouts and their guns went off to war, probably not to be seen for six months—the period of their enlistment. The older men kept singing until the sun was up. Then all the Indians went home lonely for their young men. Their fathers and mothers and wives felt grief and fear. The Chiricahuas had just killed four Apache-Mohave scouts, but they dared not cry for that could bring bad luck. They must bear the sorrow in their hearts and hope for success and many spoils from the enemy.

I had nothing to do the next day so I went around the agency and visited the different camps of the Apache-Mohaves. Most of the camps were on the south side of the Gila River where only cacti and a few cottonwood and mesquite trees grew. White men were using so much water up stream that little flowed through the river where the Yavapais had their fields. Instead the water stood in puddles—called tanks—from which the people irrigated their crops. My people still lived in the little round thatched huts that I remembered from my boyhood. But the huts were covered with canvas instead of animal skins to keep out the cold.

James Roberts went with me. I was just like a white man among my own people. I could not speak to them in their tongue. The Indians did not know me. One old man told James Roberts that I was his son. But I knew better and returned to my tent.

The next day I stayed home. Several women with children came to visit me. James Roberts was with them. One woman called out, "Hoomothya." She was Cealiah, my cousin who had often looked after me with her own younger brothers and sisters—many years earlier when we all lived together in the Salt River Canyon. She had escaped alive from the cave where our parents were slaughtered. She explained how she had been spared. At dawn of that terrible day, she and five other young women went to the pits where the mescal was cooking as it was time to take it out. Cealiah was the daughter of my aunt who had died in that cave with three of her children and with my own little brother and sister. She was the daughter of the uncle who had abandoned me at the campfire to be captured by the enemy—if he had not I would not be alive today. Cealiah said she had learned that I had been captured by soldiers on a trip with her father, and she had often wondered if I still lived.

Cealiah was married to the son of a noted chief of the Verde River band of Apache-Mohaves, named Jut-a-ham-a-ka (Chicken Neck), who later became a great medicine man. I did not meet Jutahamaka at this time because he was an enlisted scout who had just gone out and would not be back for at least two months.

When the people in the Apache-Mohave camp learned who I was, many women and old men came to see me. They began to cry when they saw me for they had long given me up as dead. When they saw me, it made them think of olden times. I came back like a ghost from the dead dressed in different clothing. I listened carefully to everything they were saying to me, and soon I was speaking my own language again.

A few days after my arrival at San Carlos, an old friend from the Fifth Cavalry visited me. Captain John Bourke was for many years an aide-de-camp of General Crook. I had not seen him since the Sioux war of 1876. Bourke told me about Mrs. Burns' death. He advised me to write to her children who were then grown up and tell them that Captain James Burns had adopted me and I was one of their family. In that way I might have some share in some property belonging to the Burns' family. But Bourke forgot to give me their address in Washington D. C.

Bourke was a writer and wrote much about General Crook's life and his Indian campaigns. At this time he wanted to learn all he could about Indian ways. I helped him with much of this writing, and he promised that when the book was finished and sold, I would get my share of the money. I went to a great deal of trouble inviting many Indians to tell me their stories about how they used to live and about their principal foods. Several years after his visit—I never did see him again because General Crook was soon replaced by General Miles—I learned that he died at San Antonio, Texas. I never got anything for helping him with his book, which is called *On the Border with Crook*.

When the detachment I stayed with was ordered to join their company at Fort Elliot, Texas, I was assigned to the Indian company stationed at the agency. An Indian named Captain Snooks was the first sergeant. I stayed with the Indian company until I was discharged from the United States Army on January 26, 1886.

After my discharge I moved to my cousin Cealiah's camp across the river about one-half mile from the agency. She had three grown girls and two small boys.

I waited about a month for my army pay and my mileage allowance from Fort Leavenworth, a distance of over one thousand miles. I had a hard time getting the mileage money. The pay officer said that Indian scouts were never paid for mileage when they were discharged from the service, and he did not approve the mileage allowance due me. So I wrote a letter to my old friend General Crook who was still commanding the Army in Arizona. I informed him I had been denied my rights as a soldier in the United States Army and asked him to see that I was allowed my mileage claim. About two months later, a letter came telling me to go to Fort Thomas and receive payment. I boarded the first stage to Fort Thomas, a distance of about thirty miles, and gladly signed the receipt for ninety-seven dollars. I never heard from General George Crook after that. He went off to Omaha to command the Department of the Platte, and General Miles became the commander of the Department of Arizona.

A few months later, Captain Edwin Pierce, the acting Indian agent, called me to his office and asked me what kind of work I could do. I told him I could do carpentry, painting and farming and that I had a teaching certificate from Highland Academy in Kansas. Captain Pierce hired me at two dollars and fifty cents a day as a carpenter to repair the school house. After I finished repairing it, Captain Pierce kept me at work getting children from the camps and putting them in school.

There had been no school for the San Carlos children for nearly three years because of the Chiricahua War. So, I went to the different camps urging the old folks to send their children to school. I told them education was the making of a man or woman. Some parents refused to send their children because the government had made so many false promises to them. They claimed that some of their children had been sent East to stay for three years, and it was now eight years since they had seen them. It was hard at first to get any children to come to school, but soon some older children agreed to come.

I was in charge of the Apache-Mohave and Apache-Yuma boys. Another educated young man named Robert McIntosh was in charge of the San Carlos and Coyotero Apache children. McIntosh was the son-in-law of Eskiminzin, the well-known Arivaipa chief whose tribe was massacred near old Camp Grant.

Not long after the school started, Mr. Watkins was hired as the superintendent and his daughter as a teacher. We got along very nicely until the Apache Kid—another son-in-law of Eskiminzin—and his band raided the agency. Most of the children ran off to their camps, and the school was closed for that year. Robert McIntosh went back to his camp above the Gila River. I was without a job.

33
The Apache Kid
May 1887 — November 1889

In September 1886, Geronimo, twenty-four warriors, fourteen women and children, several Apache scouts and sixty or more troublesome Chiricahuas were loaded on a train headed for Alabama. My people thought that the soldiers had everything under control and we soon could return to our own country near the Verde River. In the spring of 1887 when all was going well for me, more troubles began mostly because of the Apache Kid.

Has-kay-bay-nay-ntayl, later known as the Apache Kid, was born on the San Carlos Reservation. The few times that I saw him, he appeared to be about my age, so he must have been born about 1865. He was a White Mountain Apache, a member of Captain Chiquito's band, who were not wild and troublesome Indians like many other Apache tribes. When he was a young boy his family lived in Globe where he got to know many white men who called him the Apache Kid. There the Kid met Chief of Scouts Al Sieber who took a liking to the boy and made him his helper. Apache Kid took on many of the white men's ways, just like I did. He learned English and dressed in white men's clothing. He usually wore a black sombrero and boots. When he was old enough the Kid became an Apache scout.

The Apache Kid got along well with Indians and white men. He accompanied Al Sieber on many scouts, became a sergeant in 1882, and accompanied General Crook and Sieber on the Geronimo campaigns. About 1885 he married a daughter of Eskiminzin. In May 1887, while I still had a teaching job at the San Carlos school, Captain Pierce and Sieber went to Fort Apache to check the situation out there. Sieber left the Kid in charge of the scouts and the guard house. Liquor got the Apache Kid, just as it got other uneducated Indians into big trouble.

Just as soon as Captain Pierce and Sieber were on their way, Apaches in a camp up river brought out the drinks and began a celebration. Sergeant Kid and his men went to the camp to break up the festivities and destroy the liquor, but they forgot their duties. Instead of breaking it up, they joined the party that lasted for a week. When an Indian was killed at the camp, the scouts were in no shape to arrest the murderer.

Soon after Captain Pierce and Sieber returned to headquarters, Kid and his men, still drunk, rode up to Sieber's tent. Sieber scolded them for disobeying orders and took away their weapons. Captain Pierce ordered them locked up in the guardhouse. Soon an excited crowd of Apaches gathered nearby; someone fired a shot; a bullet hit Sieber's ankle; and another whizzed by Captain Pierce's head. During the commotion, Kid and his scouts escaped and headed in the direction of Mexico.

Two Fourth Cavalry Troops were soon in pursuit of the renegade scouts, and a courier hurried off to Globe and brought back Doctor T. B. Davis to attend Sieber's wounds. When General Miles got word of the trouble, he left Los Angeles for San Carlos. The Apache Kid, who had not done anything bad yet, returned to San Carlos and surrendered on June 25, 1887.

At the court martial held in Globe in June, all the witnesses including Captain Pierce, except Sieber, said that they did not see Kid armed or shooting at anyone, that he did not even resist arrest until all the shooting began. But Sieber, who was still hurting from his wound, held the Apache Kid—the boy he had always treated as a son—responsible and charged him with assault and intent to kill. He charged Say-es, Hale, and Pash-ten-tah as accomplices. The four scouts were convicted and sentenced to ten years at Alcatraz Federal Prison.

A few months later, a federal court decided that civil courts, not the military, should have settled the matter and that these Indians were being held illegally. The Kid, Sayes, Hale, and Pashtentah went back to San Carlos. By this time Captain John Bullis had replaced Captain Pierce as Indian agent, and Sieber was walking with a cane. Sieber still blamed the four scouts, especially the Apache Kid, and in October a warrant for their arrest was granted.

Sheriff Glenn Reynolds and Deputy Ryan caught the Kid and his companions and arrested them. The Apache Kid denied that he or the others did the shooting, but Al Sieber and five others testified against them. The jury found the Kid and his accomplices guilty of the intent to kill, and Judge Kirby sentenced them to seven years in the Yuma Territorial Prison, a punishment most people considered worse than immediate execution. Few prisoners left that prison alive; they died slowly of consumption.

Sheriff Glen Reynold's job was to get the Apache Kid and seven other convicts to Yuma. Reynolds refused Sieber's offer of an escort of Indian Scouts. This was the biggest mistake the sheriff of Gila County ever made—and his last. The convicted men were placed on a stage for a two day journey to Casa Grande where they were supposed to board a train to Yuma. The Kid and Hos-cal-te were considered the most dangerous and were handcuffed and their feet shackled to the coach. Six others were handcuffed. Only Jesus Avott, a young Mexican sentenced to two years for stealing a pony, wore no irons at all. The driver, the sheriff and the deputy were all well armed. On the second day when the overloaded stage reached a steep, winding hill. All the party except the driver and the two men who wore leg irons proceeded to walk up the hill. The other prisoners except Avott were hand cuffed in pairs. The sheriff made the big mistake of allowing the prisoners to follow him. They attacked and killed him and his deputy and released the Kid and Hoscalte. Avott escaped to a ranch where he reported the prisoners' escape. Middleton, the driver was shot through the neck, but he walked to the nearest town where he told the story of how the Apache Kid had kept the others from finishing him off. A rare snowstorm covered the tracks of the now heavily armed Apaches, and they disappeared into the wilderness.

Soon Arizona's greatest manhunt began. Every military post in Arizona was notified. Gila County offered a reward for each convict caught. After Sheriff Reynolds' murder, every theft and every murder of every white person or Indian in central and southern Arizona was blamed on the Apache Kid. The Arizona Territorial Legislature offered a five thousand dollar reward for him, dead or alive.

34
Echawawmahoo's Ghost Dances

A Yavapai medicine man named E-cha-waw-ma-hoo (Enemy's Head) used to roam the Bradshaw, Bill Williams and San Franciso Mountains. In 1873 General Crook forced Echawawmahoo and his people to live on a reservation near Camp Verde, where Cottonwood and Clarksdale are now, and kept them under guard. Two years later, about the time I left Arizona, the white men forced Echawawmahoo's people, the Apache-Mohaves to move to San Carlos to live with the real Apaches—the Pinals, the Arivaipas, the Coyoteros, and later the Chiricahuas.

Echawawmahoo was a lonely man with no close relatives and lived with a cousin who later became my father-in-law. One day in early spring of 1888, Echawawmahoo began to act strangely. He went off for a whole day, ate some green grass and returned to the camp with flowers. At dinner time, he refused to eat anything, saying he was not hungry. For a whole month, he left the camp each morning before anyone was awake and returned after everyone was in bed. When anyone happened to see Echawawmahoo, he was looking up and moving his lips without making a sound. We all worried about him, so we asked a man named Shai-haw to speak to him.

One evening after Echawawmahoo lay down, Shaihaw went to him and asked what was wrong and why he never ate the food that was offered him. Echawawmahoo said he had eaten all he wanted and his stomach was always full. When Shaihaw asked him where he got food to eat, Echawawmahoo said that the Great Spirit fed him. Shaihaw was astonished at all the medicine man told him.

Echawawmahoo told Shaihaw to summon all the Apache-Mohaves to Chalipun's camp for a great medicine dance that would begin at sunrise the next morning. Chalipun's band was the first Yavapai band to surrender to General George Crook at Camp Verde in 1873. Chalipun's real name was E-jach-ta-shun-a (Big Hat). His large camp was located near a spring called Coyote Hole, nine miles northwest of the San Carlos Agency and about half way to Globe.

Each band chose a young man and a young woman to lead them to Coyote Hole. Each young man carried a stick with a cross at the end and a cloth tied to it. In the center of each cross was a small looking glass. The maidens were dressed all in white with white eagle feathers in their hair. Two young men beating small drums followed the leaders. These drums were made from two-gallon buckets containing water and covered with flour sacks secured with strong strings. The tops were coated with flour and water and rubbed until smooth and tight.

Many Apache-Mohaves—men and women, young and old—followed the drummers in single file. When they reached Chalipun's camp, almost everyone saluted the medicine man as they walked close by, but no one dared touch his person. When the people were seated, the four maidens sprinkled pollen on their heads.

When the opening ceremony was over, the medicine man told the people that the Great Spirit had led him to another world and had taught him many things. He was sent back to his people to tell them the great news. "This world will soon change," Echawawmahoo said. "If all the Indian people will listen and do as they are told, the Great Spirit will restore our land to us, and he will send a plague to the white people who will vanish from the earth. When the Indians get their land back, food will be ready to eat all the time."

The medicine man ordered the ghost dances to begin that very night at sunset, and messengers hurried to the agency to tell the other Indians. Almost everyone went to the dance. Echawawmahoo sat at the center of the camp near the large fire. The great medicine man was adorned with white feathers and yellow stuff painted all over his face. I went to the dance, but I did not get close enough to make any bow to the supposed great medicine man. Shaihaw said, "If anyone in our midst does not have great faith in the purpose of dancing, he will cause failure. In order for the dance to bring success, we must believe that a great change is coming." We were also told that we must dance until sunrise, but some other young men and I stole off and went home early.

I went to the next dance that was held near the Apache-Mohave camp of Marshal Pete. I did not wish to dance. Even when several pretty young girls came up and asked me to dance with them, I always refused. Finally, several girls grabbed my arms and dragged me to the place where others were dancing. I had lived with white people so long that I was not familiar with my people's dancing. I did not know the tunes and had a hard time keeping in step with the beating drums. But the young maidens kept pushing me on. I wanted to go back to my comrades, but the girls kept me there in the middle of the ring. Every time I tried to get away, two girls held my arms. I was held that way nearly all night.

Finally, the singing and the beating of the drums stopped. Then, we were told to fire a volley up to heaven as a sign of joy. I got out of there. I found that I had hardly any shirt left. The shirt I had bought to wear to the dance was torn to shreds. The next morning, I had to buy a new one.

Toward the end of April when the days were becoming hot, dusty and sultry—while Apache Kid and his ten followers were out causing trouble—a great earthquake shock startled the Indians all over the San Carlos Reservation. Many who had doubts about what Echawawmahoo had said, now believed him. They now believed that big changes in this world would soon happen.

The medicine men told the people to come together to start dancing at a certain place for thirty days. "Then," he said, "the Great Spirit will appear in person to the Indians and will restore all their land. All the white people will vanish from the Indians' land, and the dead and long-forgotten Indians will come to life and join their relatives and will never die again."

About a week after the earthquake, I received word to come to Coyote Hole for a feast and spiritual dancing. I soon learned that most Tonto-Apaches, Apache-Yumas and Apache-Mohaves had gone to Coyote Hole to the place where Echawawmahoo, the medicine man, stayed, and many agency employees and United States Indian scouts had joined the frolic makers. All these Indians believed that if they did not do as the medicine man said, they would be punished the same as the white people when the Great Spirit of God appeared.

I did not go to the ghost dances. A few days after the dance near the camp of Marshal Pete, Captain Bullis who had replaced Captain Pierce as the San Carlos agent found

me employment with Doctor Poughborn, a farmer hired by
the government to help the Apache-Mohaves who lived
along the Gila River. I worked every day. Doctor Poughborn often asked me why I had not gone to Coyote Hole
with my people. I told him that I believed that if the world
came to an end and every living thing perished, I would not
be spared no matter what kind of man I was.

I stayed on working with Doctor Poughborn until
Captain Bullis offered me a better job. Bullis could not
speak the Yavapai language, and there was no one at the
agency to interpret for the Indians. He wanted me to take
the job as interpreter. My pay stayed at two dollars and fifty
cents per day. That job suited me very much. I had only to
sit in my chair all day as there were few Indians around to
interpret for. When I had been at the agency for about a
week, several Indians came back to draw their rations and
then left again. During all these days the Apache Kid and his
renegades were still at large.

Some Indians left Coyote Hole and camped on the
other side of the river. Just as I reached their camp late one
afternoon, five young men arrived with several bronco ponies. They were going up the San Carlos River, a tributary
that empties into the Gila right at the agency. Casaldo the
head chief of the San Carlos Apaches was having a great
dance there. This ingenious old chief had a peach orchard,
and he sold peaches to everyone who came to his camp. The
young men with the ponies said that all the Indians assembled at Coyote Hole were coming to the dance. One young
man caught a pony for me to ride, and we rode off toward
Casaldo's camp about twelve miles away.

When we were still some distance from the camp, we
heard the beat of the drums. We arrived at the camp about
dusk, tied our ponies to some thick brush a short distance
from the dance and went over to the fire where several men

and women were gathered. The medicine men were singing, and four men were beating drums.

After many people, who came from a greater distance than we, arrived all at once, the dancing began in earnest. A few minutes later, we heard gun shots from the hills above us. We paid no attention to the gun fire until someone came into the crowd shouting that the Apache Kid was shooting at everyone he came across and was coming in our direction. When we heard more shots that seemed closer, everyone began to leave the dance. When I got to my horse, he was so frightened that he kept jumping and pulling on the rope. I could not get the rope untied and decided to leave the horse. Just then I saw a friend about to mount his horse, and I asked him if he had a knife. He tossed me the knife. I cut the rope, released the horse and called to my friend, but he had already gone. I soon overtook him and returned the knife.

A party of at least fifteen hundred Indians had been frightened by a party of eleven men. Many Indians had guns with them, but I was not able to protect myself because I was unarmed. As we rode down the river, we passed many people, some riding and some on foot. Some begged to let them ride up behind us. But my companions advised me not to mind their pleas and to look out for myself. I returned home after midnight and had a few hours sleep.

Some dancers hid out in the brush and did not return to their camps until morning. Many left their horses at the place where they had tied them. When they returned, they found not only their own horses but their friends' horses too. Many women from Coyote Hole had left their horses and walked fifteen miles on foot. Their friends returned their horses to them. A few young women went home with young men they had not known before. There were no complaints. They got married and are still married today.

Later, we found out that the Kid was not in the area. We laughed with one another about the great flight we had made. Some said that Indians drunk on tizwin mixed with whiskey had done the shooting. Others said that Indians living near the camp did not care to have such a gathering there and scared the crowd away with the shooting and making everyone believe that the bad Apache Kid was near. Everyone was afraid of the Kid.

About a week after the big scare, my people attended another great dance at Coyote Hole. Many Indians came to Echawawmahoo's lodge carrying their firearms. At midnight each man with a gun came forward and placed it in a row pointing east. While the men were doing this, the medicine man held up his gun, fired it in the air, turned the muzzle downward, and as everyone watched, a melted substance fell from the gun. "This," Echawawmahoo said, "is what will happen to the soldiers' guns if they come to bother us. Their bullets will not hit the Indians, but our bullets will hit the white men. The Indians will be helped by the Great Spirit who will make the white men's guns useless. Our enemies cannot harm us, if you stay with me." I think these Indians who went to the ghost dances would have had great trouble if they had followed the advice of the medicine man, Echawawmahoo.

35

General Nelson Miles and the Yavapai Chiefs

The farmers employed by the government to take charge of the Apache-Mohaves' farms came to the agency and reported that they could not find any Indians in their camps. They wanted them back to clean the ditches and build a strong dam, but they could not find any Indians to do the work.

The government farmers could not persuade Captain John Bullis to force the Indians back into the fields. Captain Bullis was not a young man who had just come into the service from West Point. He had been in the Army for many years, and he considered things a long time before he took action. If he had been a quick-tempered man, he would have ordered the soldiers, the Indian policemen and the scouts to gather up all the Indians who had abandoned their camps, their farms and their crops and had been dancing for two months.

Several years earlier, Indians had performed ghost dances at the camp of an Apache medicine man named No-ca-del-klin-ny on Cibecue Creek. Troops attacked the dancers, and the Indians started a rebellion. Captain Bullis said to the government farmers, "The Indians are having their time out to have dances. Let them alone, and they will come back to their farms when they get tired of dancing. Their legs will not hold out forever. Just look out for yourselves, and do not worry if there are no Indians on the farms right now. Your salaries will go on just the same."

Captain Bullis was right. Many Indians came in from Coyote Hole where the great powwow was in progress. They came in to draw their weekly rations of flour, sugar, coffee, and beans. Some families returned to their own camps to stay. They became tired of the way they had been living—always hot with no protection from the sun and always hungry. They were tired of the quarreling among themselves. One day word came that the spring at Coyote Hole was nearly dry. The tribes would soon move away to another larger spring..

Before the Apache-Mohaves could move from Coyote Hole, General Nelson Miles, the commander of the Division of the Pacific with headquarters at Los Angeles, came to the San Carlos agency. Someone had told him about the Indians leaving their homes and their fields to have ghost dances. I was at the agency the day the general arrived, and we recognized each other at once. He wanted to see the Yavapai chiefs at the agency, and he asked me to be his interpreter. General Miles came to San Carlos not to punish the Indians but to listen to their appeals so that he could report their wishes to the President. General Miles asked me to send out messengers to the main camp and all the other camps telling the chiefs to come to him the next day.

I sent a runner to Coyote Hole where nearly two thousand Indians were assembled. He arrived at the camp early in the morning while the crowd was still dancing. As he rode swiftly into the camp, the dancing stopped. The messenger then called the names of all the chiefs and ordered them to come into the agency by ten in the morning to have a talk with the soldiers'great chief, General Miles. He told them if they did not come, there would be great trouble. The various San Carlos Indian tribes were separated into bands, and each band had its own chief. The Apache-Mohave chiefs were Ma-quaw (Quail's Horn) of band A, Way-poo-da-doppah (Little Flat Block) of band B, Marshal Pete of band C, Paw-cuel-lah (Long man) of band D, Quan-a-thack-haw (Green Leaf) of band E, Ka-pet-yu (Turtle's Egg) of band F, Paw-chine (White Spots on Forehead) of band G, and Sta-gol-lah (Crooked Mouth) of band H. The two Apache-Yuma chiefs were José Coffee of A band, and Captain Snooks of B band. Chalipun was the head chief of all the Tontos and commanded A, B and C bands.

All the chiefs except Maquaw, who was old and crippled, arrived on time for the meeting. Maquaw's nephew Way-ga-high-a (Wet Back) represented Band A.

The first chief to speak was José Coffee of the Apache-Yumas. This was the same Pakotay whom I had known at Date Creek—the man I wrote about. "I went with General Howard to Washington in 1870 to meet with President Grant," José Coffee said. "I agreed at that time not to shoot soldiers. I wanted my people to be brothers to all white men. But now all my young people have gone almost crazy over dancing. For that reason I want to go away from here. If there is any trouble over the dancing, I do not want to be any part of it."

"You are a good chief," said General Miles, "a good friend to your people and to the white men. You and I must have many talks." José then asked General Miles for a pass to leave the reservation and visit some of his people who had never been to San Carlos but who had made their homes on the bottom lands of the Gila near Mohawk and Agua Caliente.

The next chief to speak was Marshal Pete, an Apache-Mohave chief. "I have talked to all classes of white men," said Marshal Pete. "I told them about the promise that General Crook made to my people when he returned to Arizona after Geronimo had started the war against the white men. General Crook said, 'You have always listened and tried to do things in the right way. You have worked your land and dug ditches and dammed the water. I want the Apache-Mohaves and the Apache-Yumas to be an example to the other Apaches.' Then, General Crook said, we would be more respected and get more help from the government, and we could return to our farms on the Verde River. Geronimo and all the troublesome Chiricahuas are now in Alabama, and my people are still living in a place they do not call home."

General Miles said, "I am very sorry to tell you that General Crook could not do all that he had promised. He has no more power than any Indian. He could only ask the government in Washington to help you. Of course General Crook may have already asked the government to send the Apache-Mohaves, the Apache-Yumas and the Tontos back home. And it might be that the government did not approve General Crook's request for your return. Now, it is too soon after Geronimo made so much trouble for the people in Arizona. It is a bad time to get everything you want. Also, the people in Yavapai County do not care to have you move back there where you used to roam. They think it is too soon for you to be civilized.

"Nevertheless, it is true that you have been a great help to the government in the war against the Chiricahuas. I feel sympathy for you and will do all I can to get the government to send you back to your homes. I can not say how long it will take to get an answer to my request from Washington. I will send a long letter telling about the promises General Crook made. It will add to your favor when I tell how most of you enlisted in the army to fight the Chiricahuas."

I believe that no one should promise anything without true facts and the authority. General Crook should not have made such promises to my people without having the power to do so. General Miles had to leave for Los Angeles that night, but he promised to meet the chiefs there. General Miles asked the Apache-Mohave chiefs to choose men from their people to visit their former homelands. Lieutenant James Waterman Watson and a company of the Tenth Cavalry were detailed to go with a party of Apache-Mohaves and Tonto-Apaches to Fort McDowell, to follow the river to Camp Verde, to go from there to Fort Whipple, and finally to cross the deserts to Fort Mohave and the headquarters of the Department of the Pacific at Los Angeles. Lieutenant Watson was told to keep written records of what the Indians thought about the land

General Miles chose José Coffee, Sam Kill and me to go directly to Los Angeles, and he ordered Captain Bullis to supply us everything we needed for the trip. It was during this trip that José told me about his journey to Washington with General Howard twenty-five years earlier. The three of us traveled for two days and one night by military ambulance to Fort Grant, received rations for the remainder of our journey and continued on another light wagon to the railroad station at Wilcox. We arrived at that little rough town at noon and stayed there until after dark when we boarded a train going west. Arriving at Yuma the next morning about eight o'clock, we had time for only a cup of coffee before we were on our way again.

An officer met us at the Los Angeles station and escorted us to quarters near the headquarters building. While we waited for General Miles to call for us, we went to Santa Monica Beach and saw the Pacific Ocean. We watched the tide come in and saw people filling baskets with sea shells. On the third day we had a talk with General Miles. José

Coffee asked the general to persuade the government to let him go back to his own country. "Many Apache-Yumas," José said, "are living on the Gila River just above its mouth on the Colorado River. They have lived there many years and raise corn, wheat, barley, watermelons, pumpkins and other crops. These people are free to do as they please, and they get along well with the white people who live nearby. Many Indians work in the mines and are paid the same as other laborers." José wanted the government to let him and his people go to the Gila River.

General Miles then directed us to take the train back to Yuma and from there to go up the Gila River and look over the valley that José talked about, visit with the people, and have conferences with them before returning to San Carlos.

When we reached Yuma, Mohaves from Fort Mohave met us and helped us carry our stuff across the bridge to the Apache-Yuma camp where we visited the chief. Here I received a message from General Miles to return to Los Angeles. He needed me to be his interpreter.

So I said good-bye to my two comrades, loaded my little baggage on the ambulance, and headed back to Yuma. Two days later, I arrived in Los Angeles where I waited for nearly a week for Lieutenant Watson and his party of Apache-Mohave and Tonto chiefs to arrive. Watson reported to General Miles about the lands that they had visited. Watson said that the people of Waypoodadoppah's band wanted to go to Fort McDowell; Quanathackhaw's band wanted to live in the valley near Camp Verde; and the other four bands wanted to move to their old farm lands on Clear Creek below Camp Verde, on the headwaters of Beaver Creek near Montezuma's Well, and on Oak Creek. There, they said, was more farm land than at San Carlos.

General Miles said he would send Lieutenant Watson's report to the President of the United States and to the Secretary of the Interior for their consideration. He also promised to recommend that the Apache-Mohaves be allowed to return to their former homes.

General Miles did not know how long the government would take to respond

Before I left Los Angeles, General Miles gave me a note to give to the commanding officer. The note authorized me to enlist as a scout in the Tenth Cavalry.

36

Chasing the Apache Kid
and Other Wild Indians
July 1888 — July 1889

When I returned from Los Angeles to San Carlos, I joined Chief José's company of Apache-Yuma scouts. One and a half months later, the parties with Lieutenant Watson arrived telling of their visit to their former homelands in the Verde Valley. They were eager to get news from Washington allowing the Apache-Yumas to move to the country near Date Creek where Congress is now, the Apache-Mohaves to Fort McDowell and the land near Camp Verde.

Captain Bullis said he could not say when we could leave San Carlos. We might have a long wait before the President could sign the papers. He said in time the Indians would have to look out for themselves and do what they should without being told. They would not live on reservations but with white people. Captain Bullis then ordered the Indians back to their farms—to work on the ditches, build dams and irrigate their fields—so they would have something to live on while they waited to return to their former homes.

During this time of waiting, I sometimes worked as a scout and sometimes assisted as an interpreter for the agency. The Apache-Yumas and the Apache-Mohaves speak the same language—a dialect of the Yuman tongue. The Coyoteros, Arivaipas and the Chiricahuas—the real Apaches—speak an Athapascan language. When the Apache-Yumas and the Apache-Mohaves speak to a white man or to the real Apaches they need an interpreter.

One day a runner came to the agency and reported that a party of Indians had killed a white man on the San Pedro River across from the Indian camp. Apache Kid and his gang were the chief suspects. I joined Lieutenant Watson, about fifteen scouts and a company of soldiers. We made camp on a headwater of Deer Creek below the coal field. The next morning a white man led us to the place where the man had been killed, but the body had disappeared. We were unable to find tracks because all kinds of animals had been there since the killing five days earlier.

The guide who took us to the killing place said, "A white man came to the San Pedro settlement with some whiskey and began to drink with the Indians. After a few days many Indians became very drunk, went off, came back with guns, and shot the man. The other Indians left the San Pedro River camp and returned to San Carlos." That is all he could tell us.

We scoured the country for three days without finding a trail. As we followed an old wagon road toward another Indian camp on the Dripping Spring Wash near the Gila River we met an old Indian woman. She said that she had come from San Carlos to the camp on the San Pedro River where her people were—the camp toward which we were headed—but when she arrived at the camp, no Indians were there. So she spent the night there alone. Lieutenant Watson asked her if she had heard about the killing on the San Pedro River a few days earlier. She seemed frightened to hear the news, but she said she knew nothing because she had been away. I told her that Lieutenant Watson wanted her to accompany us to her village. Lieutenant Watson thought she knew something about the shooting affair, and he told me to keep an eye on her.

In the evening we came to the camp on the bank of the Gila River at the mouth of Dripping Springs Wash. We saw large fields on both sides of the wash where wheat, barley and corn had been harvested recently. We made camp at the site of the abandoned camp. Corn was drying on the roofs of the shades and huts, and the windows of the larger huts were fastened with wire. Lieutenant Watson ordered us to open up the huts and search everywhere for belongs of the dead white man. We ransacked every hut and found nothing belonging to any white man. But it did not look right that they had left so suddenly, leaving most of their own valuable belongings behind. Were they frightened because their people had done the murdering or had someone come and told them what had happened?

The next morning we followed the trail of the Indians from the Dripping Springs Camp. The trail led over the Mescal Mountains, a range of the Pinal Mountains, and across a very rough canyon. In a few hours, as we stopped for a short rest, we saw smoke curling over the mountain side. We quickly mounted our horses and hurried up the mountain. From the top of the mountain we saw two Indians leading their horses down the other side. They did not appear to see us. We waited until they were closer to the smoke and then hastened down the mountain side. I soon came to a steep gulch, and when I peered into it I saw a large camp with many huts. When Lieutenant Watson arrived, he ordered us to move right into the camp. We were expecting a fight, but the Indians did not seem to mind us coming near them. Lieutenant Watson ordered all the Indians to assemble for a talk and to be counted. The chief said that he had a paper giving him permission to stay away from the San Carlos Reservation. He and his people had been away from the reservation for nearly ten years. They had never done any harm to white men or other Indians but had been peacefully working their farms.

I was with Lieutenant Watson's company until January 26, 1889. That was the last time I served with the United States Cavalry. While I was with him we marched many miles hunting down the Apache Kid's gang with no luck at all. In March 1890, Watson's men fought a big battle with Kid's gang of renegades in the Salt River Canyon. Many of the Kid's gang were killed, but the Apache Kid's body was not among the dead. Lieutenant Watson was promoted to captain for reducing the size of the Kid's band.

The Apache Kid was blamed for many murders; but it never was certain, which, if any, he actually committed. Sometimes other rough and wild Apaches broke out, and their bad acts were blamed on the Kid. White outlaws often made their crimes look like the work of Indians. Many times, the Kid's death has been reported but never with much proof, and no one knows where or when he died or of what cause. He may still be alive today.

Six years after the Apache-Mohaves and the Apache-Yumas had met with General Nelson Miles and visited the land to which they wished to move, the Yavapais began to leave San Carlos. In 1894 Chief José Coffee and the Apache-Yumas moved to Mohawk, Palomas and Agua Caliente Springs.

Three years later, more than twenty years after my people, the Apache-Mohaves, had left the Verde River valley, Chief Marshall Pete called us together. "We are free to leave; now we can go home," he said. "If we don't go now, the government will send us to Oklahoma or another place far away. I say let's go. I have already greased my wagon, and I am leaving here early tomorrow morning. Whoever wants to go home, follow me."

So Chief Pete and the Apache-Mohaves started back to their old country near Camp Verde, the place they had been forced to leave in 1875 about the time I left Fort Whipple to fight in the Sioux Wars. I went with them. Only a few Yavapais who had married Apaches stayed behind.

My people went home. They left all their houses and their cattle, sheep, chickens and turkeys and their fields and their crops behind. Going home meant more than all the houses and cattle and chickens and crops in the world. I had given up a career in the Army and a farm in Ohio, but at last I was back home in the land of my mother's people.

The Verde River Flowing Through Fort McDowell

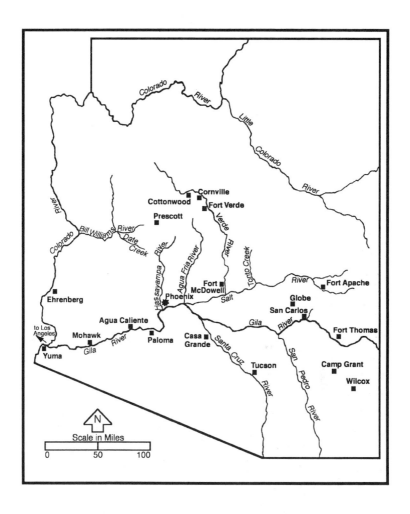

From San Carlos to
Yavapai Lands 1894-1900

Epilogue
Mike Burns at Home
on the Verde River
1897 – 1934

Mike Burns' manuscript ends abruptly with little explanation of his move from San Carlos to the Verde River and no description of his life thereafter. However, through his correspondence with Dr. Carlos Montezuma and Sharlot Hall and from the writings of his contemporaries, we have fragmented sketches of his later life.

Where Mike first settled after leaving San Carlos is not clear; but in a letter to historian and author Sharlot Hall, dated March 7, 1923, Mike wrote that he came to Mayer, Arizona, in 1900 and remained there until moving his family to Fort McDowell in 1910. From letters to Dr. Carlos Montezuma, we learn that Mike at times lived in the Cottonwood area, in Mayer, in Prescott and at Fort McDowell.

When in 1900 the Yavapais arrived at Fort McDowell, they found Mexicans and white Americans farming the lands where they had expected to settle. The Indians stayed alive by doing odd jobs, begging and sometimes stealing the farmers' corn, melons and other crops.

In the autumn of 1900 a government inspector reported to the Bureau of Indian Affairs that eight or ten

Apache-Mohave families were living at the abandoned military reservation. The inspector recommended that unsettled land at Fort McDowell be reserved for the Indians who then with a little help could take care of themselves.

During the autumn of 1901, Dr. Carlos Montezuma—his Indian name was Wasaja—returned to the land of his boyhood. He, like Burns, was an Apache-Mohave who had lost all his family during the Yavapai War. Montezuma had not seen his homeland since his capture by the Pimas in 1871. He subsequently had been purchased, baptized and adopted by Carlos Gentile, an itinerant photographer. During his thirty year sojourn in the East he had become a Christian, a physician and a strong advocate—writer and speaker—for the cause of all Native Americans. During his 1901 visit, the first of many, he became acquainted with his Yavapai relations, including Mike Burns. Mike had corresponded with Montezuma before the visit, and this relationship would continue for many more years. For twenty years Montezuma would provide financial and vocal support for the small Yavapai community at Fort McDowell. Montezuma's correspondence, which includes letters from Mike Burns, may be found at the Department of Archives and Manuscripts, Arizona State University.

On September 15, 1903, the Fort McDowell Apache-Mohave Reservation became a reality. President Theodore Roosevelt signed a document setting aside the land of the abandoned fort—except that which had been legally settled by others—for the Apache-Mohaves living nearby. In 1904 the fifty-eighth Congress passed an act enabling the Secretary of the Interior to purchase land within the bounds of the reservation from the settlers having lawful claims.

The Yavapais' troubles continued. For over twenty-five years, the white men tried to move them to the Salt River Reservation to live with the Pimas. Through the efforts of Chief Yuma Frank, Charles Dickens, Mike Burns, Carlos

Montezuma and others, the Yavapais retained their land at
Fort McDowell.

In his letter of April 30, 1914 to Montezuma, Mike
Burns described his life at that time. He began by thanking
Montezuma for the enclosed dollar bill that came just in
time to buy "sugar and coffee for myself and my family."
McDowell, Burns wrote, "is the loneliest place I have ever
lived. There is no way to get work in order to earn money
enough to get something for my family. No telling how I
could get through this winter if I had no friends who helped
me along. I have been called to attend U. S. Courts as to be
an interpreter twice now. Once I was up near my home as it
was at Prescott and once at Phoenix. My services for being
interpreter is five dollars per day. Only had six days' pay at
each place and expenses paid. J. P. Dillon who is the recent
U. S. marshal is the one who gets me that job. I have known
him for the last twenty years, and whenever I meet him, he
always hands me five dollars to buy something for my children...."

Al Fenn, after interviewing Burns' daughter Mrs. Lula
Smith, wrote, "Mike Burns became well known in Arizona.
He was the official interpreter in Arizona courts. He had
many close friends among the white people including former
Judge and Governor Raymond R.C. Stanford at whose
home he spent many a night when he was in the city.... At
Fort McDowell, Burns was postmaster and wrote short
stories about the Indians...." Fenn's article, "Story of
Mickey Burns, Another Great Apache—Survivor of Mas-
sacre Cave," is part of the Arizona Collection at Arizona
State University.

In his letter of April 30, 1914, Mike listed his children
as Solomon, Carlos, Kattie, Charlotte, Lula and Josephine
Burns. He referred to his wife as Hattie Burns and himself
as Michael Burns, a Mohave-Apache Indian from
McDowell. In an earlier letter of December 1913 to Monte-

zuma, he listed his children's ages as fifteen, seven, six, five and two. The oldest must have been born about 1898 and the youngest early in 1914.

"The chief Yuma Frank has not been well for a long time," Mike continued, "but since the weather has been warm, he is getting somewhat better. And we all hope to see him out again to talk for the Indian cause here. This little band of ours needs much help here. We are going to make talk to some one for claim on this state for settlement to the land of Arizona, which was taken away from us without treaty."

Mike was apparently over his old hatred as he wrote, "I have not seen the Pimas nor Maricopas yet." Two weeks earlier, on April 19, 1914, Burns had written a letter to Montezuma on behalf of Pima chief Juan Andresa of the Salt River Agency.

On September 12, 1914, Mike wrote from Prescott, "So I am up here at the U.S. court. Many men to be tried for selling whiskey to the Indians." He discussed the proposed dam on the Verde River. In a later letter dated April 17, 1919, Mike criticized the Phoenix Indian School's abusive treatment of children. At that time four of his children attended that school.

About the turn of the century Mike's former cave home and the bones of his murdered family were rediscoverd. The site became known as "Skeleton Cave." Both Montezuma and Mike visited the cave. In 1925 as a result of Mike's petition, the remains of his family and the other victims were moved to the Fort McDowell cemetery.

In 1921 Dr. William Corbusier, Mike's childhood friend from Date Creek Camp, visited him at Fort McDowell. Corbusier found the Yavapais living there slightly more prosperous than those remaining at San Carlos, whose condition was little improved from 1875 when they had first arrived there. "Most of them," he wrote, "were living in

round huts made from boughs of cottonwood trees and
thatched with grass, old canvas and pieces of tin. They slept
on the ground. Some had ragged blankets, but most pre-
ferred to sleep directly on the ground, as less likely to attract lice. They cooked mostly in tin cans or over an open
fire. They had learned to speak English, and a few had some
schooling."

"Even at McDowell," Dr. Corbusier wrote, "there were
many old, nearly blind women, who had lost their menfolks
during the wars, eking out an existence by making blankets.
They received only a pittance for them, possibly seventy-
five cents for one that sold for eight or ten dollars in the
stores."

For many years Mike Burns worked on what he called
The Indian Version of the Arizona Yavapai Wars, telling
how his people were wronged by the white men. He also
wrote about the first thirty-two years of his own life. Hoping to publish his manuscript, containing hundreds of pages,
he sent parts or all of it to publishers and friends. In a letter
to Sharlot Hall, dated January 6, 1910, Burns asked for "the
address of a man or a magazine paper to whom I can send
letters to about a little history of the Apaches? and including
my own history." It is not known if Sharlot Hall provided
him with addresses, but extracts from his manuscript appeared as early as 1915 in Thomas Farish's *History of Arizona*.

One person acquiring sections of Burns' manuscript
was Dr. William Corbusier, with whom Mike had corresponded for several months before the doctor's visit to Fort
McDowell in 1921. Corbusier wrote, "He had not been able
to take proper care of his manuscript and it was in rather
bad condition.... After it had been transcribed and arranged,
I went over it with him and made what corrections he de-
sired and started enlarging his history and accounts of the

Indian wars in Arizona. It was quite a task at my age, and the completion of it will have to be left to others."

The doctor's youngest son, William T. Corbusier, wrote, "Mike entrusted what was left of his manuscript about the Yavapai Indians of Arizona to Dr. Corbusier. After many laborious hours and infinite patience, the story was whipped into fairly presentable shape. Many publishers were approached, but none was sufficiently interested to risk the expense of publication. That was before the great wave of western lore swept the country. Since then, this writer with his father and after his death, alone, has worked on it from time with the hope that its historical value will be sufficiently recognized to warrant publication."

In a letter to Sharlot Hall, dated April 28, 1923, Mike wrote, "I had received your kind letter a few days ago and was glad to get your answers in regard to my manuscripts. I have about 247 copies already typewritten and only waiting publication...." Mike briefly described Dr. Corbusier's visit and lack of success in having the writings published in New York or Boston. He requested a meeting with Sharlot Hall to discuss his manuscript and "what we could do about it." Mike's original letters to her may be studied at the Sharlot Hall Museum in Prescott, Arizona.

In *Verde to San Carlos*, William T. Corbusier, quoting his father's notes and his mother's letters, described the Yavapai culture and related their history. Stories about Mike's early life—including sections missing from the existing manuscript and especially about his life at Camp Date Creek—appear in Corbusier's book. One chapter is titled "Hoomoothya." Nothing about Mike Burns' life after Date Creek, except their meeting nearly fifty years later, in 1921, appears in *Verde to San Carlos*. The Corbusiers' acquaintance with the young Yavapai was limited to those few months at the soon to be abandoned camp.

Mike Burns must have been talked about frequently among the four Corbusier boys of whom William T. is the youngest. Mrs. Corbusier wrote from Camp Grant in 1886, "I was never quite sure what happened to Willie when he appeared one day with a bleeding wrist. The boys [Phil and Frank] insisted that he had been made a blood brother of Qua-tha-hoo-a-hoo-ba (Yellow Face) and christened Hoo-moothya or Wet Nose...

"For a number of years Willie was called by this name whenever his nose became troublesome, though the proper translation of the name did not apply to his kind of wet nose."

"Hoomoothya, finely translated," William T. Corbusier wrote, "means 'wet and moist around and on the nose.' It has no reference to a dripping or runny nose. When Mike was born the moisture was like sweat."

"Willie," wrote William T. Corbusier (about 1962) "still carries the 'absurd little scar' on his left wrist and likes to think he was christened Hoomothya after Mike Burns, the original."

The seven hundred or more existing pages of Mike Burns' writings contain many repetitions and gaps—most likely the result of assistance by many editors and loss through distribution of sections to others. Listed in the bibliography of *Verde to San Carlos* is "Burns, Mike, 1922. Manuscript owned by W. T. Corbusier." However, Mike Burns apparently continued to write or rewrite his story. One segment of his manuscript is dated 1929, Fort McDowell. An original manuscript is in the archives of the Sharlot Hall Museum in Prescott, Arizona and copies are at Arizona State University in Tempe, Arizona, the Fort McDowell Library and elsewhere.

Louis Miner wrote in the obituary column of the *Prescott Evening Courier*, November 26, 1934, "Mike Burns, colorful Mohave-Apache, who recently underwent hospitalization at Whipple, is no more. He died yesterday and was buried this afternoon on the Fort McDowell Indian reservation....The death of Burns marks the passing of one of the state's most colorful characters, and his deeds during the hectic days of frontier life will go down in Arizona history. Throughout his life Mike Burns was known as a wise counselor to his people, and his loyalty will be a watchword among the hosts of friends wherever he was known."

Mike Burns is buried near his relatives, victims of the Salt River Cave massacre, in an unmarked grave in the Fort McDowell cemetery. Many of his descendants reside today at the Fort McDowell Reservation.

Memorial to Victims of the Salt River Massacre

Ft. Darwell. Arizona. April. 30th 1914

To Dr. Carlos Montezuma.
7 W. Madison St. Chicago Ill.

My dear cousin Gus.

Your welcome letter was just handed to me to-day. and also to my surprise, when open it to read, found a dollar bill. I was so pleased, as it come just in time to buy me. some sugar and coffee for myself and family. This is the loneliest place, I have ever lived. as there is no way to get work in order to earn money enough to get something for my family. no telling how I could ever get through this winter: if I had no friends who helped me along. I have been called to attend U.S. courts: as to be interpreter. twice now. once I was up to near my home: as it was at Prescott and once at Phoenix. my services as being interpreter: at $5.00 per day: only had 6 days pay. at each places: and expenses paid:

J.R. Dillon. who is the present U.S.
Marshall. he is the one gets me that job.
at U.S. Courts. I have known him for the
last twenty years: and whenever I meet him
he always hands me $5.00 to buy something
for my children. as he called my baby girl.
attached to his name. instead: Joe: as his name
he calls her Jossie; or Josephine Burns.
I will write down my childrens names. -
first Soloman Burns. Carlos² Burns
Kattie³ Burns. Charlottie⁴ Burns Juls⁵ Burns
and Josie Burns. the mother of them Hattie Burns
and the father or myself Michael Burns.

Mojave Apache Indian McDowell.
The chief Yuma Frank. has not been Well for a long time
but since the Weather has been warm. he is getting
some What better. and We all hope to see him out
again; to talk for the Indians's cause here.
This little band of ours: need much help here!
and We are going to make a talk to some one. for
claims in this state for settlement to the land of
Arizona. which was taken away from us. with out
treaty. I have not seen the Chews nor mercopes yet
So hoping to hear from you again. Sir: I am your cousin.
                    Michael Burns.

Carlos Montezuma Collection, in the Arizona Collection,
Arizona State University Libraries, Tempe Arizona

J . DILLON

Cigars, Pipes, Tobaccos and Smokers' Articles

LAWLER BLOCK

Prescott, Arizona, Jan. 6th 1910.

Miss Sharlot M. Hall

Phoenix Ariz.

Dear Friend:

Pardon me madam, but as a friend of mine has given me your address and in the line of your work on about the history of Arizona and its people Mr. Jolly. the Supt. of the County Schools. And probably you have met him once or have also heard of him As to make known to you. I am an Apache Indian of this Territory. and received a little education at Carlisle Indian School of Penna. Give you gave me the address of a man or a magazine paper. to whom I can send letters to. About a little history of the Apaches? and including my own history. As I was captured by the U.S. Soldiers. When I was only 8 years old. in the year 1872. near Four Peaks. or if you still writing for some papers: Can you help me? I will await for your reply as soon as possible.

Remains yours truly

Mike Burns

In care of J. P. Dillon

Prescott Ariz.

Fort Mc Dawell Ariz.
April. 28th 1928

To Miss Charlotte Hall.
        Dewey. Ariz.

Dear madam.

I had received your kind letter afew da
ago. and was very glad to get your answer. in regards to
my manuscripts, I have about 247 copies. already typed
and only waiting for publication. I wanted to go to these
at the time of 4th of July. or if not. I may be at Pioneers
in Sept. But I will try to be there on the 4th of July.
I had an old army Officer friend. whose name is
Col W.H. Corbusier U.S.A (retired) He tried to have
my manuscripts to be printed in book for me in New Yk
and in Boston. but he said. that he could not find any
Book publishers to handle it. and says those Eastern
people care very little about Indian stories. and also
says. that the publishers. say. there will be no sale for
such books. enough to pay for publishing Indian stories.
I would like to meet you in person. having all of my writing.
and for you to see for yourself. what we could do about it.
I used to lived at mayer. spent about 17 years there. knew
all the old timers. Joe mayer was a personal friend of mine
William Murphy I used to farm at his place at mayer
I have some water right on that farm. and I wanted I
go up there some day to see about it.

        So please answer me again soon.

Very respectfully Mikel Burns

Bibliography

Altshuler, Constance Wynn. *Chains of Command, Arizona and the Army, 1856-1875.* Tucson: Arizona Historical Society, 1981.
_____*Cavalry Yellow and Infantry Blue, Army Officers in Arizona Between 1851 and 1886.* Tucson: Arizona Historical Society, 1991.

Alynn, Joseph *Pratt. Arizona of Joseph Pratt Allyn: Letters of a Pioneer Judge.* edited by John Nicholson. Tucson: University of Arizona Press, 1974.

Bender, Averam. *A Study of the Western Apaches,* 1846-1886. NewYork: Garland Publishing Company, 1974.

Bourke, John. *General Crook in Indian Country.* Lincoln: University of Nebraska Press, 1891.
_____*On the Border With Crook.* New York: Scribner's, 1902.

Brown, J. Ross. *A Tour Through Arizona: Adventures in Apache Country, 1864.* New York: Harper Brothers, 1871.

Burns, Mike. Manuscript. Prescott, Arizona: Sharlot Hall Museum, 1923.
_____Letters to Sharlot Hall. Prescott, Arizona: Sharlot M. Hall Collection, Sharlot Hall Museum.
_____Letters to Carlos Montezuma. Tempe, Arizona: Arizona Collection, Arizona State University Libraries.

Carr, Camillus. *A Cavalry Man in Indian Country, 1865.* Ashland, Oregon: Press of Lewis Osborne, 1974.

Conner, Daniel Ellis. *Joseph Reddeford Walker and the Arizona Adventure.* edited by Donald J. Bethrong and Odessa Davenport. Norman: University of Oklahoma Press, 1956.

Corbusier, W. T. *Verde to San Carlos.* Scottsdale, Arizona: Dale Stuart King, 1971.

Crook, George. *General George Crook, His Autobiography.* edited by Martin F. Schmidt. Norman: University of Oklahoma Press, 1960.

Eason, Nicholas J. *Fort Verde, an Era of Men and Courage.* Sedona, Arizona: Tonto Press, 1966.

Farish, Thomas Erwin. *History of Arizona.* 8 vols. San Francisco, California: Filmer Brothers, 1915-1918.

Fenn, Al. "Story of Mickey Burns, Another Great Apache Survivor of Massacre Cave", article in Arizona Collection. Tempe: Arizona State University, September 30, 1971.

Gibson, Arrell. *The Oklahoma Story.* Norman: University of Oklahoma Press, 1978.

Hayes. Jess G. *Apache Vengeance: True Story of the Apache Kid.* Albuquergue: University of New Mexico Press, 1954.

Henson, Pauline. *Founding a Wilderness Capital: Prescott, AT, 1864.* Flagstaff, Arizona: Northland Press, 1965.

Howard, Oliver O. *My Life and Experience Among Our Hostile Indians.* New York: De Cape Press, 1972

Khera, Sigrid, Editor. *The Yavapai of Fort McDowell.* Fountain Hills, Arizona: Fort McDowell Mohave-Apache Indian Community, 1979.

Khera, Sigrid and Mariella, Patricia. "Yavapai"; Opler, Morris. "Chiricahua Apache"; Basso, Keith. "Western Apache"; Ezell, Paul. "History of the Pima" in *Handbook of American Indians: Volume 10, Southwest.* Smithsonian Institute, 1978.

King, Charles. *Campaigning with Crook.* Norman: University of Oklahoma Press, 1964.

Miner, Louis. Mike Burn's obituary in the *Prescott Evening Courier*, November 26, 1934. Prescott, Arizona: Sharlot M. Hall Collection, Sharlot Hall Museum.

Schreir, Jim. "The Skeleton Cave Incident." Phoenix: *Arizona Highways*, May 1991.

Schroeder, Albert. "A Study of Yavapai History" in Horr, David Agee. *Yavapai Indians*. New York and London: Garland Publishing Company Inc., 1974.

Thorne, Kate Rutland. *Yavapai: the People of the Sun*. Sedona, Arizona: Thorne Enterprises Publications, Inc., 1993.

Thrapp, Dan. *Encyclopedia of Frontier Biography*. 3 vols. Glendale, California: The Arthur H. Clarke Company, 1988.

_____*Al Sieber, Chief of Scouts*. Norman: University of Oklahoma Press, 1964.

Waterstrat, Elaine. *Commanders and Chiefs: a short history of Fort McDowell, 1865-1890*. Fountain Hills, Arizona: Mount McDowell Press, 1993.

Wells, Edmund. *Argonaut Tales*. New York: Frederick Hitchcock, 1923.

Index

About the Author

Elaine Waterstrat grew up in Hemlock, New York and graduated from the University of Buffalo, majoring in history. After marrying Rod at West Point on graduation day, she taught in public schools in New York, Kansas, Virginia, Arizona and overseas and raised three children.

After Rod's retirement, they settled in Fountain Hills, Arizona, which is adjacent to the Fort McDowell Yavapai Reservation. Elaine spent many hours during the past 11 years researching the Yavapais and their interactions with white men and other Indians in 19th century Arizona Territory. She is the author of *Commanders and Chiefs: A Brief History of Fort McDowell, Arizona (1865-1890)*.

Elaine and Rod Waterstrat
The Verde River and Mount McDowell are in the background
Photo by Henning Haggblom